Marketing Your Invention, Product, or Journey

Fourth Edition

DAVID D. POSTOLSKI

AMERICAN BAR ASSOCIATION
Intellectual Property Law Section

Cover design by Jill Tedhams/ABA Design

Printed in the United States of America.

29 28 27 26 25   5 4 3 2 1

Discounts are available for books ordered in bulk. Special consideration is given to state bars, CLE programs, and other bar-related organizations. Inquire at Book Publishing, ABA Publishing, American Bar Association, 321 N. Clark Street, Chicago, Illinois 60654–7598.

www.shopABA.org

Contents

Preface

Some 3,000 years ago, shoemakers and scribes marketed their services on clay tablets. Ancient Greeks used town criers to proclaim the arrival of ships full of wine and spices. Today, businesses market to potential customers with attractive business signs, pamphlets, brochures, billboards, radio and TV communications, telephone solicitations, door drops, commercial text messages, email advertisements, banners and pop-ups, rich media advertisements, and many other marketing and advertising tools. Some things will never truly change but marketing has changed! The way one markets their inventions or products has come a long way. Using television and radio will always be a staple but with the advent of social media, new marketing outlet contenders have emerged. How potential consumers obtain their information has also changed. Marketing is now in the palm of your hands or in your ears and it's all in an instant! Content is king but it still needs its guard to protect its court. Some of these new marketing outlets have become less expensive as content comes directly from the inventor or creator. However, that too may come at a price when taking into consideration intellectual property laws and other regulatory schemes. Social media has made everyone a critic and such instant criticism can make or break your invention or product. They said bad news is also good news but in a sensitive cultural environment like social media that age old saying may not hold true today. Instant successes can happen from just the perfect marketing storm but that may mean ruin can happen just as fast too! How you spin your story may turn the tides, but it also may not. Today, we are living in a digital age, which means inventors and entrepreneurs need to not only protect their brands but also think about their reputations and image while garnering and maintaining their customers' loyalty. This book is dedicated to how we market our inventions, products, and companies. Each chapter and author will explore a new age in a marketing outlet. Each author has unique experiences in their respective marketing outlet so sit back and enjoy the read.

With new marketing outlets and technologies comes legal and ethical considerations that need to be explored as well. A marketing strategy must complement your IP strategy! So let's begin there!

About the Editor

David Postolski, a partner at Gearhart Law, is a registered patent attorney and intellectual property (IP) attorney for close to 20 years. David specializes in assisting inventors, creators, artists, startups, entrepreneurs, early-stage companies, and emerging companies with their U.S. and international IP strategy, protection, enforcement, and monetization. David is a frequent speaker and author on emerging IP issues and technologies, including raising capital, AI, business formation, food science, software, licensing, data and privacy compliance, equity-based crowdfunding, and compliance with other U.S. and international regulatory structures. David is also a professor at Temple University, Parsons School of Design, and the Radzyner Law School (Herzliya, Israel) where he teaches master-level students about IP, ethics, and other regulatory considerations. David is a current Council Member of the American Bar Association Section of Intellectual Property Law, founder of their International Action Group, editor of their monthly newsletter, and the outgoing Continuing Legal Education (CLE) Officer. David currently serves on Harvard's Lemann Entrepreneurial Program Advisory Board.

About the Authors

Elizabeth Gearhart has a PhD in chemistry and works at Gearhart Law, a full-service intellectual property firm; she worked as a patent agent then moved to marketing, where she uses her research skills to optimize the marketing effort for Gearhart Law. She's currently starting a podcast consulting business. She, her husband Richard, and Kenya Gipson co-host a nationally syndicated radio show for entrepreneurs called Passage to Profit: Road to Entrepreneurship. They interview inventors on the show on a bi-weekly basis. The show is recorded in Manhattan at the iHeart radio studios and is released as a podcast the day after it airs on the radio. The show is in its seventh year. She also co-hosts The Jersey PodCats podcast with Danielle Woolley, where they invite cat lovers to share issues that the community can come together to solve.

Richard Gearhart is the founder of Gearhart Law, founded in 2006 to serve entrepreneurs by providing patent, trademark, copyright, and IP litigation law services, as well as education. Richard has been an intellectual property attorney since 1990, is the managing partner at Gearhart Law, and currently is a member of the Rutgers Health Leadership Council. Richard co-hosts the nationally syndicated Passage to Profit: Road to Entrepreneurship radio show and podcast with his wife Elizabeth and Kenya Gipson. Richard commands a breadth of experience that comes from nearly 30 years of practice in the writing and prosecution of hundreds of patents, and in all aspects of IP law. In 2022, Richard was recognized by ROI New Jersey as a 2022 ROI Influencer in the Law List category for being one of the best of the best in New Jersey for intellectual property law.

Kenya Gipson is a wife, mother, and passionate wellness advocate. Struggling with her health after a difficult pregnancy and excessive weight gain, she decided to become her wellness advocate and began a personal mindset and health transformation through running. As a four-time marathoner and certified coach through The National Academy of Sports Medicine, she developed E.A.S.E. (Energizing, Active, Strength, Exercise), a wellness format that helps transform negative thought patterns and develop a healthy body and mental state through movement and mindfulness. Movement and mindset are the key ingredients this "Marathon Mama" used to achieve her 50-pound weight loss; and it's the same recipe she teaches in her weekly fitness classes and on her nationally syndicated radio segment and podcast, Power Move. Kenya is the host of MEternal, a podcast and platform (meternal.info) on iHeartRadio dedicated to creating awareness about the black maternal health crisis and access for multicultural mothers to create healthier outcomes in communities of color. Kenya's wellness journey has been featured with NIKE and on *The Today Show*. Her mission to master motherhood, marriage, and media is what motivates Kenya to optimize her full potential by living a balanced lifestyle and empowering other women to do the same.

Andrew Ive founded Big Idea Ventures to help solve the world's biggest challenges by supporting the world's best entrepreneurs, scientists, and engineers. Andrew is responsible for investing and building companies across technology sectors, including food and agriculture. Andrew works with investors, corporations, and governments to invest and build the most transformative companies and ecosystems around the world. Andrew built the world's first food tech accelerator in New York City, investing and supporting young food companies globally. Andrew is a Harvard Business School graduate and an advisor for the Tufts Nutrition Council and the Friedman School of Entrepreneurship; advisor to the Founder's Institute in Zurich; mentor to the Food Tech Accelerator in Italy & Oxford Entrepreneurs in UK. Andrew has started and grown many companies and began his career in brand management with Procter & Gamble.

Emily Kenison is a lawyer turned inventor and CEO of Emikeni Inc., which has led award-winning product innovation, building brands that redefine women-led inventions. Emily is the founder of Straplets (www.straplets.com), the first and only detachable shoe accessory, and RobeCurls (www.robecurls.com), the award-winning heatless hair curler. With seven awards in product innovation, her inventions are regularly featured in top publications and on television, including in *Vogue* and *Glamour* and on the *Today* show. She holds 12 patents, 9 trademarks, and over 100 copyrights that support her continued ambition to inspire the future of women entrepreneurship. Driven by sustainable design and the love of people, her companies are members of WBENC, 1 percent for the Planet, and Climate Neutral Certified. Follow the journey on emikeni.com and learn more about her inventions at www.robecurls.com and www.straplets.com.

For more than 25 years, **Scott Krady** has advised law firms, consulting firms, venture capital groups, technology, banks, asset managers, and early-stage and emerging high-growth companies on go-to market strategies. Working alongside executives and investors, he has led the design and execution of innovative market strategies, including brand development, thought leadership, communications, business development, operations, and intellectual property. Scott has a demonstrated track record of accelerating revenue growth and brand visibility for organizations in energy, consumer, retail, financial services, healthcare, professional services, and across technology including fintech, SaaS, and cybersecurity.

Yannis Moati has a rich background of 15 years in travel, from guiding tours in Europe at a young age to co-founding an exotic travel agency, and then directing a New York-based global tour operator company. Throughout his professional life, for both his clients and personal travels, Yannis had to always pull strings to get more personalized hotel check-in or check-out times. Frustration turned to illumination, witnessing firsthand the important customer behavioral shifts of the "on-demand" economy: something could be done in boosting hotel revenues by selling uncommitted inventory by day. Yannis gathered some of the hospitality industry's brightest to form HotelsByDay.

Chris Rawley is the CEO of Harvest Returns, a platform he founded in 2016 to democratize investments in agriculture. The company has funded over $40 million in farms, ranches, and agribusinesses across the world, while giving investors a streamlined way to connect with the food system. Rawley is a retired Navy Reserve Captain. During his 30-year military career, he served in a variety of leadership positions in naval, expeditionary, and joint special operations units afloat and ashore. He deployed to Afghanistan, Iraq, throughout Africa, the Middle East, and the Western Pacific. Rawley has a degree from Texas A&M University, earned an MBA at George Washington University, and is a graduate of the U.S. Naval War College. He is the author of *Unconventional Warfare 2.0.*

Chapter 1

Marketing Your Invention

An Overview of the Legal Issues in Marketing

David D. Postolski

Intellectual property (IP) refers to intangible assets such as inventions and designs that are covered by patents; literary works, music, art, literature, and other creative and artists' works covered by copyright; words, logos, and symbols that are covered by trademarks; and the increasingly important trade secret. IP is the exclusive monopoly one is awarded or granted by the U.S. government (or any country) over the physical embodiment of one's ideas. IP is the power to control your intellectual efforts as property. IP is your journey's or company's single most important asset and value, so protecting it at all costs is super important. However, having a great invention or product is not enough. It is not "build it and they will come." Once protected, all inventions and products must be supported by great marketing. Navigating how IP law intersects with marketing is a topic on which we must be educated and empowered to ensure certain legal rights are not lost to your invention or product.

IP is a territorial right. Whatever country you file in is the county where your IP is protected. If you want protection in the United States then obtaining a U.S. patent, trademark, or copyright is your goal. The same goes for any other country in the world. Having IP allows you to market and sell your product in a specific territory with the peace of mind that in the event infringement occurs you have the ammunition to go against a particular infringer in a particular territory where you already have the registered right. As a brief overview, the four types of intellectual property include patents, copyrights, trademarks, and trade secrets, all briefly described in the following sections.

PATENTS

In addition to being able to create, market, and use your innovation, a patent gives you the power to exclude others from creating what you created, marketing what you market, and using your innovation without a license to do so. When you receive a patent, it typically lasts for 20 years if the patent pertains to the utilitarian features of an invention that is based in science (chemistry, biology, physics, computer science, mechanics, electronics, etc.). There are also patents that are based in design and those last 15 years. Computer-generated graphic symbols, screen displays, graphic user interfaces (GUIs), and even web pages may be protected by design patent law.

COPYRIGHTS

Copyright refers to the form of intellectual property protection that safeguards the creative and artistic works of original works of authorship, which may include music, art, literature, and other genres. Copyrights also cover the architecture and software of computers as embodied in their software code. Copyright protections are automatic, that is, whenever the creator, author, or artist creates something, the copyright is automatically there. All that is needed is to register their work with the U.S. copyright office to have maximum protection. Creative and artistic content may include written material, photographs, art, graphics, the layout of an advertisement, music and videos, and website designs. A person's identity, such as his or her name, photograph, image, voice, or signature, may be protected by publicity or privacy rights, an offshoot of copyright and constitutional law. A copyright lasts the entire life of the creator, artist, or author plus 70 years after they are deceased.

TRADEMARKS

A trademark is a distinctive source identifier that distinguishes your goods or services and can be any term, phrase, symbol, design, smell, or taste or combination thereof. A trademark serves as the primary means that consumers identify your business, goods, and services offered in the marketplace. Distinctive packaging, like the shape of a bottle or container, may also be protectable as a trademark, industrial design, or, in some countries, as a trade dress. Trade dress refers to the manner in which a product—or place of business—is "dressed up" to go to the market. It is the totality of elements in which a product or service is packaged or presented. It may include features such as size, shape, color or color combinations, texture, graphics, or even particular sales techniques. Technological developments have enabled the creation of new and more creative marks. Animated/moving image marks and sounds, for example, are particularly suitable for marketing and advertising and are ideal for today's marketplace—the internet.

TRADE SECRETS

A trade secret is the secret sauce or something that gives your business or venture its competitive edge. Trade secrets can include distribution methods, sales methods, consumer information, customer lists, algorithms not publicly disclosed in a patent, advertising campaigns and strategies, lists of suppliers and customers, and production procedures. Your trade secret protection lies in treating and keeping this competitive advantage as a secret to everyone under nondisclosure agreements. The moment it is disclosed this protection is lost.

Marketing is all about disclosure! Any marketing strategy involves appealing to your potential customers and your existing consumers. That usually means truth and transparency. Given IP laws, saying or revealing too much before you are protected may cause disastrous eventualities. Competitors are likely to copy and use your IP for creative inspiration, so protecting your IP first, before exposing it, is crucial.

For example, in order to obtain a patent, an invention must be "new" or "novel." This means that an invention must not have been disclosed, in most countries, to the public prior to the filing of a patent application. If your business has conceived a valuable invention for which it wishes to obtain a patent, you should abstain from any marketing efforts or disclosures of information relating to the invention prior to filing a patent application. When you market your products in an advertisement and the description of the product discloses its innovative qualities, such a disclosure will most likely bar you from obtaining patent protection, unless the national patent law provides for a "grace period." Thus, a patent application should be filed before you disclose your invention in the United States because if an inventor discloses their invention before they are patent pending then they only have one year from their earliest public disclosure to file for a patent application. In most other countries such as the European Union (EU), a public disclosure before a patent application is filed is not permitted under law. In the EU, the first time you disclose your invention must be to the EU patent office. Thus, marketing your invention before you are patent pending may give you a one-year grace period in the United States, but it simultaneously statutorily and legally blocks you from the filing in a region like the EU.

For trademarks, in many counties, the first to file their trademark application usually has the presumption of validity. Sure this presumption can be rebutted, but marketing one's trademark before clearing and filing your trademark may mean that someone could file before you after seeing or hearing your successful marketing campaign. Dealing with someone who has filed before you when you could have filed your trademark first is a problem that can easily be avoided. Similarly, your trademark and your domain name may be inextricably linked. In this scenario, registering your trademark as a domain name before someone else does is also a crucial step before launching a marketing campaign!

The whole idea behind a trade secret is that there are no public disclosures of your competitive advantage. Thus, how you market and what you say to ensure your trade secret is not disclosed is an important strategy for protecting and securing trade secret protection. Companies must take the proper precautions to prevent the inadvertent disclosure of trade secrets. Once a trade secret is disclosed to the public, even accidentally, it will no longer be possible to protect that information. Therefore, if your marketing campaign says too much then any protection you thought you had in the trade secret is gone. Trade secrets provide no protection against those who independently obtain, reverse engineer, or develop the trade secret information. An owner of a trade secret will only be protected if there is evidence of misappropriation of your trade secret, that is, parties who may have stolen or divulged such confidential information in violation of a duty of trust or a written nondisclosure agreement. Companies should also be careful not to reveal a competitor's trade secrets in their marketing and advertisements, especially if the owner has diligently tried to keep that information secret.

When it comes to copyrights, many companies will generate their own artistic and creative content, but many will use the protected copyrighted materials of others. Using IP protected material without getting the permission of its owner—either by obtaining an "assignment" or a "license"—can have unintended consequences. One should always have a written agreement with marketing and advertising agencies as well as other independent contractors that specifies the ownership details of each element of the work that will be created. When posting unregistered works on social media, one must ensure that their creative content is original and was created first by the one using or posting it to social media! Therefore, having a registration with the Copyright Office in close enough time to when you created and/or published your original work is recommended to ensure you have the evidence needed to prove that you are being infringed. Independent contractors (unlike employees) usually own all IP rights in the works they create, even if you have paid for it, unless otherwise agreed in a written contract. A valid, written agreement is required to transfer all copyright rights to you in the work you have hired someone to do. Thus, having an executed work made for hire agreement is a best practice!

Many inventors and entrepreneurs are not creative content creators and that is okay. It takes a team to launch your invention or product and that will likely include a marketing team. Understanding ownership and legal issues when it comes to creative content that is being created on your behalf and then released publicly is a crucial step in marketing your inventions and products. Alerting the public that your creative content is legally protected by copyright and trademark law is another important step. Using the term "patent pending" or the registered TM symbol or using a copyright symbol should be done without fail. Please take note that most "free" material available on the internet is protected by copyright in some way. Just because you obtain material from the internet does not mean that you can copy or reproduce it freely. Finding the copyright owner and obtaining all necessary licenses is not always an easy task but should be part of your marketing journey.

Today, there is no excuse for using someone else's copyrighted works without first obtaining permission in what is called a license. Licenses can be free or sometimes may have a cost but the cost of not asking permission first will be indubitably more expensive to you! A license is an agreement whereby the person who owns the IP (licensor) authorizes another person (licensee) to make certain uses of the IP, under certain conditions and usually in exchange for payment. Do not assume that your use of someone's copyright is fair and falls under the legal notion of fair use. There are few exceptions as to how your use would fall under fair use, and they usually involve educational purposes or imitating a work for the purpose of parody or social commentary and making quotations from a published work. Again, such fair use exceptions are very limited and even if you use other people's work, you must attribute the work to the author as attribution falls under the copyright creators' moral rights as the original creator of the work. Attribution is not a defense to copyright infringement and should be done regardless of whether you are authorized to use the work or believe you are entitled to. Consulting an attorney as to whether your use is fair use is recommended. Free licenses of copyrighted works may be found under what is called the Creative Commons (http://creativecommons.org/). Here creators and artists can offer their rights to third parties with certain conditions. The creative commons license will have limitations on the work, but it may be a path for you to use other people's works in your marketing campaigns without legal and financial consequences.

Keyword triggering occurs when a search engine operator sells keywords to a business, so that after a web user enters those particular keywords in a search engine, advertising banners or pop-up advertisements appear along with the list of search results. This may expose both the search engine operator and the marketing and advertising company to legal liability for trademark infringement, misleading advertising, and unfair competition. Comparative advertising, by its very nature, can mislead consumers, and can unfairly discredit your competitors. There are many legislations in place that restrict comparative marketing and advertising.

Marketing your invention will at some point involve labeling your product or service. There are a multitude of laws that also define specific packaging and labeling requirements for certain products. The objective is to inform the consumer about the characteristics of the product and to protect health and safety. There are considerable differences in labeling laws of different countries so consulting a local legal expert is recommended.

Most countries allow businesses to market to children, provided a set of minimum criteria is observed. These criteria place on the marketer a special responsibility to protect children from their own susceptibilities. In addition, many countries have specific legislation for using television for marketing and advertising. For example, there may be broadcast time restrictions for particular products. Some marketing and promotional methods, such as direct marketing, unsolicited emails, free gifts, and discounts, may trigger ethical considerations as well, both for you as the inventor and for your company.

With the advent of new marketing outlets, the importance of adhering to data protection laws when marketing your inventions and products and ultimately selling your products/services is crucial. Data protection laws are legal frameworks designed to protect individuals' data from misuse, unauthorized access, and privacy violations. They establish a set of rules and standards that organizations, businesses, and institutions must follow when handling personal data. If your marketing tactics invite the collection of personal identifying consumer information (PII), such as names, addresses, email addresses, gender, and professions, be sure you protect the privacy of such information. Data fuels marketing but securing the data you collect from potential customers and consumers is crucial. Securing the marketing data you obtain from your customers and consumers is vital to ensure trust and transparency. Thus, compliance with regulations like the EU's General Data Protection Regulation (GDPR), the California Consumer Privacy Act (CCPA), and many other similar regulations is a must for marketing. National Data Protection or Privacy laws outline the need to have a clear privacy policy in place. Many countries provide for an "opt-out system" that forces a company to erase any PII they may have shared during a marketing campaign.

Corporate social responsibility (CSR) is a business approach that contributes to sustainable development by delivering economic, social, and environmental benefits for all stakeholders. In essence, it's about businesses taking responsibility for their impact on society beyond their core operations. The use of personal information raises privacy and legal concerns, but also ethical concerns that you as an inventor or entrepreneur must choose. Adopting a policy for CSR may also become an integral part of your marketing journey. All of the preceding considerations begin as early as when you first market to your potential customers.

Ethical marketing and advertising are cornerstones of the marketing industry, emphasizing honesty, transparency, and respect for consumers. Ethical marketing campaigns focus on honesty, transparency, and positive values, resonating with consumers who prioritize authenticity and responsible business practices. Marketing depends on, and celebrates, creativity. Intellectual property laws allow you to protect that invention, creativity, and distinctiveness. With the creation and use of new, advanced marketing techniques comes new issues in intellectual property law. Understanding the legal framework surrounding the business of marketing is key! Innovators, inventors, and entrepreneurs should create a detailed marketing plan that should then be shared with an IP attorney. If you are not cautious in how you market your invention or product, you can lose your IP rights or be liable for infringement of the IP rights of others. Now that the legal framework has been provided, we invite you to delve into the marketing techniques of today!

Chapter 2

Marketing Your Invention—Marketing Best Practices!

Scott Krady

Bringing an invention to market can be an exciting journey filled with challenges and opportunities. However, without effective marketing strategies, even the most innovative inventions can struggle to gain traction. In this chapter, we'll explore proven techniques and tips to navigate the intricacies of marketing your invention and maximizing its potential for success.

First, in marketing an invention it is imperative that you understand target audiences. To do so, conduct thorough market research to identify your target audience's needs, preferences, and pain points. An inventor should create detailed buyer personas to better understand your ideal customers' demographics, behaviors, and motivations. Next, tailor marketing efforts to resonate with your target audience's interests and address their specific challenges. Key is to develop a compelling value proposition and articulate it—what sets it apart from existing solutions and why consumers should choose it.

Perhaps most important is to highlight the key benefits and features of your invention that solve a problem or fulfill a need for your target audience. Once this is done, it is essential to craft a memorable and persuasive message that communicates the value proposition effectively across all marketing channels.

The foundational pieces of a marketing plan for an invention include the following:

Building Strong Brand Identity

- Develop a cohesive brand identity that reflects the personality, values, and essence of your invention.
- Design a visually appealing logo, color scheme, and brand elements that resonate with your target audience and differentiate your invention in the market.
- Consistently reinforce your brand identity across all marketing collateral, including your website, packaging, advertising materials, and social media profiles.
- Create engaging marketing content.

- Produce high-quality content that educates, entertains, and inspires your target audience while showcasing the benefits of your invention.
- Utilize a variety of content formats, such as blog posts, videos, infographics, and case studies, to cater to different preferences and channels.
- Leverage storytelling techniques to create emotional connections with your audience and humanize your brand and invention.

Using Multi-Channel Strategies

- Implement a multi-channel marketing approach to reach your target audience across various platforms and touchpoints.
- Utilize digital marketing channels, including social media, email marketing, search engine optimization (SEO), and pay-per-click (PPC) advertising, to increase visibility and generate leads.
- Combine online and offline marketing tactics, such as events, trade shows, partnerships, and direct mail, to create a comprehensive marketing strategy.

Leveraging Influencers and Partners

- Identify influencers, thought leaders, and industry experts who align with your brand and target audience.
- Collaborate with influencers and partners to amplify your reach, credibility, and brand awareness through sponsored content, endorsements, and partnerships.
- Foster mutually beneficial relationships with influencers and partners to leverage their networks and expertise in promoting your invention.

Drawing from Customer Feedback

- Solicit feedback from early adopters, beta testers, and customers to gather insights into their experiences, preferences, and suggestions for improvement.
- Incorporate customer feedback into product iterations, marketing messaging, and future development efforts to enhance the value proposition and address customer needs effectively.
- Use customer testimonials, reviews, and success stories to build trust, credibility, and social proof for your invention.

CUSTOMIZING AN APPROACH BASED ON PRODUCT

Inventions come in various forms, each requiring a tailored marketing approach. Here are some common types of inventions and strategies for marketing them:

- Medical devices or healthcare solutions:
    - Examples: Wearable fitness trackers, medical diagnostic tools, telemedicine platforms

    - Marketing Strategy: Emphasize the health benefits, accuracy, and reliability of the device or solution. Target healthcare professionals, clinics, and hospitals through targeted marketing campaigns, trade shows, and industry partnerships. Highlight regulatory approvals, certifications, and endorsements to build trust and credibility.
- Educational and learning solutions:
    - Examples: Educational apps, e-learning platforms, STEM toys
    - Marketing Strategy: Highlight the educational value, engagement, and learning outcomes facilitated by the invention. Target parents, educators, and educational institutions through educational conferences, teacher associations, and parent-focused media outlets. Offer educational resources, lesson plans, and classroom trials to demonstrate effectiveness.

By tailoring your marketing approach to the specific characteristics and target audience of your invention, you can effectively promote its benefits and drive adoption in the marketplace.

Using humor in marketing can be a highly effective way to engage with your audience, humanize your brand, and create memorable experiences. Here are some ways you can incorporate humor into your invention's marketing strategy. For example, social media content may contain funny memes, GIFs, and videos related to your invention on social media platforms. Use humor to spark conversations, entertain your audience, and increase brand visibility. Or inject humor into product packaging design with witty slogans, playful illustrations, or humorous instructions. A touch of humor can make your product stand out on the shelves and create a memorable unboxing experience for customers. In today's landscape, the most exciting campaigns are those that go viral. So, consider user-generated content campaigns, which can encourage customers to create and share funny content featuring your invention. Run contests, challenges, or hashtag campaigns that invite users to showcase their creativity and humor while using your product. Lastly, event marketing can be used to create fun and excitement related to your invention. Incorporate fun activities, games, or interactive experiences that encourage laughter and create positive associations with your brand.

Marketing your invention effectively is essential to its success in the marketplace. By understanding your target audience, developing a compelling value proposition, building a strong brand identity, creating engaging marketing content, utilizing multi-channel marketing strategies, leveraging influencer and partner collaborations, and gathering and utilizing customer feedback, you can maximize your invention's potential and achieve sustainable growth and profitability. With dedication, creativity, and strategic planning, you can bring your invention to the forefront of the market and make a lasting impact on consumers' lives.

Let's use a fictional example. In this example, we'll highlight a new invention that addresses the need for busy people to make home cooked meals. The invention, called EasyPrep, will streamline cooking time and make cooking at home easier. Here are some steps in the process of developing a marketing plan for this new idea:

1. **Understanding the Target Audience:** Market research reveals that the target audience for EasyPrep consists of busy professionals, working parents, and cooking enthusiasts who value convenience and efficiency in the kitchen. These individuals are seeking solutions to streamline meal prep without compromising on quality.
2. **Developing a Compelling Value Proposition:** EasyPrep's value proposition centers around its ability to effortlessly slice, chop, and dice fruits, vegetables, and other ingredients with precision and speed. By eliminating the need for multiple kitchen tools and reducing prep time, EasyPrep empowers users to create healthy and delicious meals with ease.
3. **Building a Strong Brand Identity:** The EasyPrep brand embodies innovation, convenience, and reliability. Its sleek design, vibrant colors, and intuitive functionality reflect the brand's commitment to modernity and practicality. The logo—a stylized knife slicing through ingredients—communicates the product's core value proposition at a glance.
4. **Creating Engaging Marketing Content:** EasyPrep's marketing strategy includes a mix of informative blog posts, engaging social media content, and captivating demonstration videos showcasing the gadget's features and benefits. How-to guides, recipe ideas, and customer testimonials highlight EasyPrep's versatility and user satisfaction.
5. **Utilizing Multi-Channel Marketing Strategies:** EasyPrep employs a multi-channel marketing approach to reach its target audience wherever they are. This includes social media advertising campaigns targeting busy professionals on platforms like Facebook and Instagram, email newsletters featuring exclusive discounts and recipes, and partnerships with cooking influencers and food bloggers to generate buzz and credibility.
6. **Leveraging Influencer and Partner Collaborations:** EasyPrep partners with popular cooking influencers and culinary experts to demonstrate the gadget's functionality and share creative recipe ideas with their followers. Influencer collaborations include sponsored content, product giveaways, and guest appearances at cooking events and trade shows, amplifying EasyPrep's reach and credibility within the culinary community.
7. **Gathering and Utilizing Customer Feedback:** EasyPrep actively solicits feedback from early adopters and customers through surveys, reviews, and user-generated content on social media. This feedback is used to identify areas for improvement, refine product features, and inform future marketing initiatives, ensuring that EasyPrep continues to meet the evolving needs of its customers.

Through a strategic combination of market research, compelling messaging, engaging content, and strategic partnerships, EasyPrep has successfully marketed its invention to its target audience, establishing itself as a must-have kitchen tool for busy individuals seeking convenience and efficiency in meal preparation. By continuously listening to customer feedback and adapting to market trends, EasyPrep remains at the forefront of innovation in the culinary industry.

In a competitive environment in which technology drives new innovation, standing out in a crowded market isn't easy. Inventors must not only have a novel idea that ideally solves a problem but must also have an addressable market that makes it viable. Though a template for success may be out of reach, there are tried and tested steps that inventors can and should take when developing a marketing plan for a new invention. By implementing these tips, inventors can create comprehensive marketing strategies that effectively promote their invention and drive adoption in the marketplace.

Here is a summary:

- **Know Your Audience:** Understand who your target audience is, what problems they face, and how your invention can provide a solution. Tailor your marketing efforts to resonate with their needs and preferences.
- **Highlight Benefits:** Clearly communicate the benefits and advantages of your invention. Focus on how it solves a problem, improves lives, or enhances existing processes. Emphasize what sets your invention apart from competitors.
- **Create Compelling Messaging:** Develop a concise and persuasive message that captures the essence of your invention. Craft compelling taglines, product descriptions, and elevator pitches that clearly convey its value proposition.
- **Utilize Visuals:** Leverage high-quality images, videos, and graphics to showcase your invention in action. Visual content is engaging and helps potential customers understand how your invention works and why they need it.
- **Build a Strong Brand:** Invest in building a strong brand identity that reflects the personality and values of your invention. Consistent branding across all marketing channels helps establish credibility and recognition.
- **Engage Your Audience:** Foster engagement with your target audience through social media, email marketing, and interactive content. Encourage feedback, answer questions, and create a community around your invention.
- **Utilize Influencers and Partnerships:** Collaborate with influencers, industry experts, and complementary businesses to amplify your reach and credibility. Influencer endorsements and partnerships can help introduce your invention to new audiences.
- **Offer Demonstrations and Trials:** Provide opportunities for potential customers to experience your invention firsthand through demonstrations,

free trials, or samples. Seeing the benefits of your invention in action can help overcome any skepticism.

- **Collect and Showcase Testimonials:** Gather testimonials and reviews from satisfied customers to build trust and social proof. Authentic testimonials from real users can significantly influence purchasing decisions.
- **Stay Agile and Iterative:** Be open to feedback and willing to make adjustments based on market response. Continuously iterate and improve your marketing strategies to stay relevant and effectively reach your target audience.

CONNECTING WITH CONSUMERS

New inventions, as with any product that aims to be successful, must connect with customers. Products need to foster emotional connections, and drive engagement with your invention's marketing efforts. Over the past decade, many new inventions have captured imagination, connected with consumers—and provided utility. Here are a few examples of recent inventions and successful marketing strategies for them.

Peloton Bike

Although Peloton Bike has recently suffered from overexpansion in a very competitive market, the company's early success is a good case study. The Peloton Bike is an indoor exercise bike equipped with a touchscreen display for streaming live and on-demand fitness classes. Its marketing strategy involved a multichannel marketing approach that included targeted digital advertising, influencer partnerships, and experiential marketing events. The company leveraged the aspirational lifestyle associated with its brand, showcasing how the Peloton Bike could transform home workouts into engaging and immersive experiences. Peloton's community-focused marketing efforts, coupled with its innovative product features, contributed to the bike's widespread adoption and success.

Airbnb

Airbnb began in 2007 and ushered in a new way of travel: the short-term rental. The company's peer-to-peer online marketplace connects users with rental listings and unique experiences. It's safe to say the company has changed the way we travel: the company has 150 million users and nearly six million active listings worldwide. But when it started, many did not understand or believe in the concept of allowing strangers to live in their homes. The company's marketing push relied on a mix of social media and guerilla campaigns focused on experiences and attention grabbing via advertising. Airbnb targeted conferences with heavy demand and where hotel availability was limited. Targeting visitors who were looking for short stays, the company booked 600 stays during Obama's

Democratic National Convention in Denver, for example. The company used sites like Facebook and Instagram, too, and exciting imagery and photography from lush locations to build a following. The company leveraged partnerships with popular travel bloggers and influencers to spread the word. Airbnb also created compelling content, such as the "Live There" campaign, which inspired travelers to "live like a local" in their destinations.

Beyond Meat

Beyond Meat launched its first products in 2012 and went public in 2019. It did so with great fanfare, fueled by shifts to healthier diets. The company's chief product, a plant-based meat alternative made from pea protein, was designed to replicate the taste and texture of traditional meat products. Beyond Meat is a good example of a marketing campaign, but the company is facing strong headwinds in the form of regulatory hurdles amid competition from domestic meat sources.

Beyond Meat employed a combination of traditional marketing tactics and grassroots advocacy to promote its plant-based products. The company collaborated with high-profile partners, such as fast-food chains and celebrity endorsers, to introduce Beyond Meat products to a broader audience. Beyond Meat also utilized social media platforms to engage with consumers, share recipes, and highlight the environmental benefits of plant-based eating. This integrated marketing approach helped Beyond Meat gain traction in both retail and foodservice channels, leading to widespread adoption and market success.

Nintendo Switch

The Nintendo Switch, a hybrid gaming console that can be used as both a handheld device and a home console, was designed to combine the portability advanced by the iPod with video games. Nintendo focused on highlighting the versatility and unique selling points of the Switch through targeted advertising campaigns and experiential marketing events. The company emphasized the console's innovative design, intuitive controls, and extensive library of games to appeal to both casual and hardcore gamers. Nintendo also leveraged social media platforms and influencer partnerships to generate excitement and anticipation leading up to the Switch's release. This strategic marketing approach, combined with strong brand loyalty and nostalgia for Nintendo's classic franchises, contributed to the Switch's commercial success.

CHANNEL MARKETING AND MAPPING TO YOUR CUSTOMERS

When marketing an invention, it's essential to utilize a variety of channels to reach your target audience effectively. These can vary based on whether you are targeting customers, businesses, or specific industries or geographies.

The advent of technology and digital channels has dramatically changed how companies market products to end customers. For that reason, we'll begin with digital marketing channels that can be considered:

- **Website:** Create a dedicated website for your invention to provide information, showcase features, and facilitate online sales.
- **Social Media:** Utilize popular social media platforms like Facebook, Instagram, Twitter, LinkedIn, and Pinterest to engage with your audience, share updates, and promote your invention through organic posts, paid advertising, and influencer partnerships.
- **Email Marketing:** Build an email list of interested prospects and customers to send newsletters, product updates, promotions, and exclusive offers.
- **Content Marketing:** Produce valuable and informative content related to your invention, such as blog posts, videos, infographics, and case studies, to educate, entertain, and engage your target audience.
- **Search Engine Optimization (SEO):** Optimize your website and content for search engines to improve visibility, attract organic traffic, and rank higher in search engine results pages (SERPs).

Despite the advent of digital marketing, traditional means such as print advertising and direct mail can still be used effectively to engage customers, and ultimately market new inventions. Key areas within traditional marketing include:

- **Print Advertising:** Place ads in relevant print publications, magazines, newspapers, and industry journals to reach your target audience.
- **Direct Mail:** Send targeted direct mail campaigns, such as postcards, brochures, or catalogs, to prospects or existing customers to promote your invention and generate leads.
- **Trade Shows and Events:** Participate in industry trade shows, conferences, exhibitions, and networking events to showcase your invention, connect with potential partners, and generate sales leads.
- **Radio and Television:** Consider advertising on radio stations or local television channels to reach a broader audience and raise awareness about your invention.

In addition, inventors may use a range of retail and other distribution channels such as marketplaces, platforms, and other third parties such as influencers and channel partners. Online marketplaces can be used to sell your invention through popular online marketplaces like Amazon, eBay, Etsy, or Shopify to reach a wide audience of online shoppers. Inventors can partner with brick-and-mortar retailers, specialty stores, or distributors to stock and sell inventions in physical retail locations. Inventors can also set up e-commerce stores on their own websites or utilize third-party e-commerce platforms like Shopify or WooCommerce to sell directly to customers online. And finally, inventors can collaborate with influencers, bloggers, industry experts, or brand ambassadors who align with their target audience and can help promote your invention to their followers and networks. They can form strategic partnerships with complementary businesses, brands, or organizations to co-market, cross-promote, or bundle your invention with related products or services. By leveraging a combination of these channels, inventors can create comprehensive marketing strategies that maximize an invention's exposure, engage target audiences, and drive adoption in the marketplace.

MARKETING AN INVENTION INTERNATIONALLY

Marketing an invention internationally requires careful planning, cultural sensitivity, and a deep understanding of diverse markets. To do so requires an additional layer of planning, including market research, as well as an understanding of a myriad of unique issues ranging from legal frameworks to local customs, which may impact consumer taste and preferences, as well as whether a viable market exists for your invention.

Here's a step-by-step guide on how to effectively market your invention internationally:

Market Research

Conduct thorough market research to identify potential international markets for your invention. Analyze market trends, consumer behavior, regulatory requirements, and cultural nuances in each target market. Evaluate competition, pricing strategies, distribution channels, and barriers to entry in international markets.

Localize and Customize

Adapt marketing materials, messaging, and product packaging to resonate with the cultural preferences, language, and customs of each target market. If applicable, translate your website, product descriptions, user manuals, and promotional content into the local language(s) to improve accessibility and appeal to international audiences. Consider cultural sensitivities, taboos, and differences in communication styles when crafting marketing messages and visuals.

International Distribution

Explore different distribution channels and logistics solutions to distribute your invention in international markets. Partner with local distributors, retailers, or e-commerce platforms with established networks and market expertise in your target countries. Consider setting up international warehouses, fulfillment centers, or partnerships with third-party logistics providers to streamline shipping and delivery processes.

Digital Marketing

Utilize digital marketing channels to cost-effectively reach international audiences. Optimize your website and content for international SEO to improve visibility in search engines across different regions and languages. Leverage social media platforms, online advertising, influencer partnerships, and email marketing to engage with international consumers and drive traffic to your website.

Event Marketing

Participate in international trade shows, exhibitions, and industry events to showcase your invention, network with potential partners, and generate leads. Research trade shows and events specific to your industry and target markets, both domestically and internationally, and plan your participation strategically.

Understand Regulatory and Compliance Frameworks

Ensure compliance with international trade regulations, import/export laws, intellectual property rights, and product safety standards in each target market. Seek legal advice and consult with experts to navigate complex legal and regulatory requirements in international markets and protect your invention's intellectual property rights.

Cultural Issues

Respect cultural differences, norms, and values in international markets and adapt your marketing approach accordingly. Avoid cultural stereotypes, offensive language, or imagery that may alienate or offend international audiences. Tailor marketing messages and visuals to resonate with the local culture and preferences while maintaining your brand identity and core values.

Seek Customer Support and Feedback

Provide multilingual customer support and localized customer service channels to address inquiries, feedback, and concerns from international customers. Gather feedback from international customers to understand their needs, preferences, and satisfaction levels, and use this insight to continuously improve your marketing and product offerings.

By following these steps and adopting a strategic approach, you can successfully market your invention internationally, expand your customer base, and capitalize on global opportunities for growth and expansion.

There are several examples of successful global marketing programs for inventions. A good one is Apple's iPhone, one of the most iconic inventions of the 21st century, and its global marketing program played a significant role in its success. Apple employed a consistent and cohesive marketing strategy across multiple countries and regions, leveraging a combination of television commercials, digital advertising, retail experiences, and product launches to create buzz and excitement around each new iPhone iteration. The company also tailored its marketing messages and campaigns to resonate with diverse cultural preferences and market dynamics, resulting in widespread adoption and success in markets around the world.

REACH AND POPULARITY

Legacy products have also put a great deal of effort and resources into their international marketing. For example Nike's "Just Do It" campaign has been a big part of the brand's broader marketing efforts. Nike has effectively marketed its products globally through high-profile sponsorships, celebrity endorsements, and innovative advertising campaigns that inspire athletes and consumers to push their limits and pursue their passions. The company's marketing efforts have helped establish Nike as a leading brand in the sports industry, with a strong global presence and loyal customer base.

THE FUTURE

Many areas—from fundraising to marketing—are constantly evolving and subject to disruption in the form of new technologies and innovative approaches. Consequently, inventors too must think "outside the box" and think about creative ways to not only market, but also to engage, delight, and interest potential customers. Social media marketing and platforms such as Instagram, Facebook, and LinkedIn will continue to be effective ways to showcase your invention and reach a wider audience. Similarly, collaboration with influencers in your industry, who have built-in audiences, will be effective at promoting your invention to large numbers of potential customers. Yet, new methods, such as crowdfunding and guerilla marketing, or activations can also be used with success. Crowdfunding campaigns can be launched on platforms like Kickstarter or Indiegogo to raise funds and create buzz around your invention. Inventors can also work with affiliate marketers to promote their inventions and earn a commission for every sale generated through their referral. Guerrilla marketing, which involves the use of unconventional and creative marketing tactics to grab attention and generate buzz, can also be used to market inventions.

Over the next decade, we can expect to see a wide range of innovative inventions across various industries. Each of them, to varying degrees, will have audiences who must engage and connect with these products before they become customers. This creates a tremendous opportunity for marketers, but also means inventors must develop a holistic understanding of buyer personas, preferences, and how their products solve problems. A few of the potential types of inventions that we may see in the next decade include sustainable energy solutions, such as renewable energy technologies, energy storage solutions, and smart grids to meet the world's energy needs in a more environmentally friendly way. We'll also see the continued evolution of AI and machine learning technologies, including autonomous vehicles, robotics, natural language processing, and predictive analytics. Augmented technologies will likely see greater adoption, leading to new applications in gaming, education, training, remote work, and entertainment. And Smart Home and Internet of Things (IoT) devices will continue to proliferate, enabling greater connectivity, automation, and convenience in our daily lives. Lastly, we're likely to experience an increasing interest in space exploration, and could see innovations in space tourism, satellite technology, planetary exploration missions, and sustainable space habitats.

These are just a few examples of the types of inventions that we may see in the next decade. The pace of technological innovation is accelerating, and it's exciting to anticipate the breakthroughs that will shape our future, creating a greater need and opportunity for marketing to ensure these products and technologies can maximize viability and deliver upon their value propositions.

For inventors, marketing will continue to be an important determinant of success. Overall, marketing is a critical component of the success of inventions as it enables businesses to reach, engage, and convert customers; build a strong brand presence; and drive revenue and growth. Without effective marketing, even the most innovative inventions may struggle to gain traction in the market. From creating awareness about an invention and its benefits to generating excitement around the invention, marketing will not only spark curiosity and generate buzz but also fuel the engine for demand for a product or service. It's important for inventors to recognize that a well-executed marketing strategy can build credibility and trust in the invention and the brand behind it, showcasing the features, benefits, and success stories of the invention. Its role is all the more important given the novelty of an invention, requiring education and product demonstration. Marketing can help play a role in facilitating the adoption of innovative inventions by explaining complex technologies in a simple and engaging way. Given the rate at which technology is altering the product landscape, marketing will play a significant role in driving long-term success for inventions. It will help sustain interest, drive customer loyalty, and support the growth and evolution of the invention over time.

Chapter 3
Harnessing the Power of the Crowd!

Chris Rawley

When developing a product, most first-time inventors quickly discover that they lack two resources. First, they may not have enough money to produce a prototype or a commercial version of their product. Hardware and software development costs are constantly on the rise, presenting significant barriers to entry to many entrepreneurs or inventors. And second, inventors generally lack an initial base of customers to buy the product they have created.

Fortunately, the internet and legislation that makes crowdfunding possible open up a world of possibilities to help entrepreneurs solve these two problems. Most people have also heard of or even donated to a charitable cause on a donor crowdfunding platform, such as GoFundMe. Because donations are generally not an accepted form of business funding, they should be avoided by for-profit companies. Instead, an entrepreneur has several other options to raise money from large crowds of people, each with their own particular benefits and drawbacks.

Reward-based crowdfunding (sometimes called social crowdfunding) offers backers of your campaign rewards, such as exclusive perks or an early version of a company's product or service. Kickstarter and Indiegogo are the most popular reward crowdfunding platforms. Several well-known products had significant early successes raising money on Kickstarter. In the spring of 2012, smart watch maker Pebble raised $10.3 million, which was then that platform's most successful offering.[1] Later that year, the makers of the virtual reality gaming headset maker Oculus Rift (later acquired by Meta) raised $2.4 million on Kickstarter to fund a very early prototype of their device. Kickstarter's main rival Indiegogo bills itself as a place "where early adopters and innovation seekers find lively, imaginative tech before it hits the mainstream."

The second way to raise capital from a pool of investors is called equity crowdfunding, which allows a company to take money from investors in exchange for equity in the business or potential future returns.

1. Interestingly, in 2016 after its second Kickstarter raise brought in $20.3 million from over 75,000 backers, Pebble ceased operation and refunded many of its backers' donations.

UNDERSTANDING EQUITY AND DEBT CROWDFUNDING

One of the first known equity-based crowdfunding platforms emerged in Australia in 2007 and was called the Australian Small Scale Offerings Board (ASSOB). Over time, ASSOB evolved into Enable Funding, a licensed equity-raising platform that has successfully raised over $150 million for 176 private companies. In the United States, the 2012 Jumpstart Our Business Startups Act (JOBS Act) established crowdfunding provisions allowing early-stage businesses to raise money from a crowd using various methods to publicly solicit investors. Since then, the JOBS Act and the rules governing equity crowdfunding have been updated several times.

Several different types of equity crowdfunding are governed by different aspects of U.S. law. Depending on which platform you choose, you may hear terms such as Regulation Crowdfunding (Reg CF), Regulation A+, or Regulation D. Equity crowdfunding is regulated by the Securities and Exchange Commission and involves many complex rules related to how much can be raised per campaign, who can invest in an offering, and how the campaign can be promoted to potential investors. Reg CF portals must be registered by the Financial Industry Regulatory Authority (FINRA). Other aspects of crowdfunding are regulated by the Internal Revenue Service and Federal Trade Commission. Needless to say, it can be a complicated subject requiring expert advice. Many platforms will refer you to a securities attorney with experience in this field to prepare your offering documents. Other crowdfunding sites will supply companies raising capital with the platform's own lawyer-prepared documents.

The number of crowdfunding platforms, the companies raising money on them, and the total amounts raised have continued to grow nearly every year since this legislation was introduced.

According to Grand View Research,[2] the global crowdfunding market size was valued at USD 1.67 billion in 2022 and is expected to expand at a compound annual growth rate of 16.7 percent to 2030. The Regulation D market is massive compared to the other types of crowdfunding, and even comparable in size to the publicly traded stock market. Data compiled by the Securities and Exchange Commission shows that from 2009 through 2020, $15 trillion of Reg D securities were sold, compared to $16.4 trillion of registered (publicly traded) securities.[3] More than half of Reg D fundraises are related to the energy and

2. Grand View Research, Crowdfunding Market Size, Share & Trends Analysis Report by Type (Equity-based, Debt-based) by Application (Food & Beverage, Technology, Media, Healthcare, Real Estate), by Region, and Segment Forecasts, 2023–2030, www.grandviewresearch.com/industry-analysis/crowdfunding-market-report (last visited Feb. 23, 2024).
3. Craig McCann, Chuan Qin & Mike Yan, *Regulation D: Issuers, Investors and Intermediaries*. Sec. & Exch. Comm'n (Sept. 21, 2023), www.sec.gov/files/craig-mccann-presentation-092123.pdf.

real estate industries, but that figure still leaves a significant amount for other types of investments.

Regulation D offerings have limitations on who can invest and how they can be solicited to the public. Whereas Reg CF and A+ offerings are oriented to "retail" investors, have restrictions on the maximum raise target, and have investment minimums as low as a few hundred dollars per investor, Regulation D offerings can raise an unlimited amount of capital. Regulation D offering investors must meet requirements related to income, net worth, and investing knowledge to be considered "accredited" or "sophisticated." Because these offerings are generally marketed toward higher net worth investors, their minimum investment level ranges from the low five figures and moves up from there. Regulation D platforms sometimes partner with broker dealers or registered investment advisors to help raise capital.

A final option some companies choose to pursue to raise capital for their product is debt crowdfunding. In this alternative to traditional bank lending, a pool of investors can loan funds directly to a startup or through an investment vehicle with terms that can vary significantly in duration and interest rate. These loans can be collateralized with real assets such as real estate or equipment, product inventory, or even accounts receivable. Several platforms specialize in these types of investments, which are sometimes referred to as private credit. Because investors are taking a risk with their capital on lending to a newly established or smaller company, the interest rates are often higher than the same type of loans would be with a bank or other lending institution.

For readers based outside the United States, the European Union and other countries each have their own various sets of regulations, but the principles provided here for fundraising from the crowd are similar regardless of specific regulations.

CROWDFUNDING IN ACTION: THE PITTMOSS CASE STUDY

PittMoss is a company from Pennsylvania that produces a unique set of products made from recycled paper and cardboard including organic potting mixes and pet bedding. PittMoss products are sold to thousands of retail consumers and over 300 nurseries and greenhouses worldwide. But like many other businesses with innovative products, the company had much more humble beginnings. Because of its water and nutrient absorption qualities, peat is very important to horticulture. Unfortunately, harvesting peat is also environmentally destructive and unsustainable. Recognizing this fact, in 1994, PittMoss inventor Mont Handley began experimenting with substitutes for peat as a soil amendment in his kitchen. He later secured a Small Business Innovation Research grant from the U.S. government that supported studies at a university to validate the effectiveness of his products in horticulture and gardening applications. Armed with the successful results of this research, in 2015, Mont and his new company PittMoss secured capital from Mark Cuban on the ABC reality TV show, *Shark*

Tank. That appearance helped PittMoss to finally launch its consumer retail product line in 2017, but the company still needed more capital to expand its business.

To solve this problem and grow their customer base, PittMoss chose crowdfunding. They decided to raise capital on Republic, a Reg CF platform with more than three million investors who have funded over $2.6 billion for startups. Over the course of two campaigns, they raised about $1 million with 2,800 new investors. Seeking additional funding, they came to Harvest Returns, the crowdfunding platform for farming and agriculture-related businesses I started in 2016. In two campaigns with us, PittMoss raised $825,000 while being exposed to more than 15,000 investors specifically interested in farming-related companies.

These campaigns provided PittMoss with not only funding but also new customers who were newly exposed to their products. The company's current CEO Brian Scott says that, "we have tried to coordinate those campaigns around our season to give us a boost with our on-line sales, hopefully get more folks asking for us at their local garden centers or big box stores, and tell their friends or family about us. So there is a lot of 'soft communication' around our company and our products that are difficult to quantify. But I know it is happening because we get some people telling us they saw us on one of these platforms."

Scott continues, "It's also important to note that often our 'perks' for investors on these Reg CF campaigns include free product that we ship for them to try (and also tell their friends about). So, we always see a spike in business when we are running a campaign, either from investors that tried it and bought more or from the spinoff sales of them telling others about us."

POSITIONING YOUR CROWDFUNDING RAISE FOR SUCCESS

When deciding whether or not to conduct a fundraising effort with an outside group of investors, a company should think about what would make its products or invention appealing to investors or backers in a crowdfunding campaign. The four most important factors to consider when deciding to launch a campaign to raise funds from the public are:

1. **Investability:** Do investors feel strongly enough about your product or company that they are willing to put their hard-earned money at risk to fund it? That is often not an easy question to answer and can involve significant introspection. Inventors or company founders tend to be passionate about what they have created, and rightfully so. Having a dispassionate outsider help you answer this question might allow you to arrive at a more truthful answer. The merits of the products or service are important for sure, but not the only consideration when you are raising capital. Angel or early-stage investors make decisions based on a variety

of factors involving emotions—like greed or compassion—as well as more tangible aspects of a product such as accessible market size and risk tolerance.

2. **Scalability:** Is your company scalable? If a company is narrowly focused around a single product, it may only appeal to a very small number of target customers. Or, is there a considerably sized market of potential users for your product or service? Total Addressable Market, or TAM, is an estimate of the total amount of the total market demand (in revenue) a company can possibly generate selling its products or services. TAM can be estimated by looking at industry data, market reports, and research studies, along with previous sales data, if available.
3. **Traction:** Do you have enough traction to appeal to investors? Traction means progress toward your company's ultimate goals. Do you have a working prototype of your invention or a minimum viable product that can be sold commercially? Have you generated sales, or is the company still pre-revenue? If you are selling a service, do you have pilot trials with paying customers?
4. **Financing:** Does your business plan support a path to profitability to ensure that investors will receive their money back? Will you need to raise additional capital in subsequent funding rounds? Even after a successful campaign, does the company have enough runway to become profitable before we run out of cash?

Some platforms will help you answer these questions to maximize your raise's success, while others are simply happy to have your fees, regardless of if you raise money or not. If you can't address these areas successfully, then your business may want to consider other alternatives to crowdfunding.

Once you've made the decision to move forward on a raise, here are six steps to follow when using crowdfunding to market your invention or startup company:

1. **Choose the Right Platform:** With over 1,000 crowdfunding platforms available to choose from in the United States, entrepreneurs should do their research and select one that aligns with your campaign's goals and target audience. Though some crowdfunding platforms will allow a company to decide if their raise will be Reg CF, A+, or D, most of them tend to specialize in a single type of offering. Reg CF raises are limited to $5 million over a 12-month period, so if a company requires more funding than that, they should consider Reg A+ (up to $75 million) or Reg D (unlimited). That said, regardless of which platform you choose, keep in mind that the average amount raised for a company on its first fundraising attempt is generally going to be considerably less than those limits. Companies should also consider the impact of bringing crowdfunding investors on their capitalization table. Reg CF raises will have more

numerous (sometimes hundreds) less-sophisticated investors, which can create a challenge from the investor relations standpoint as well as potential roadblocks to follow on funding by other sources, such as venture capital firms. There is truth to the fundraising adage that the person who invests a few hundred dollars can take just as much time and energy to deal with as someone who invests tens or hundreds of thousands of dollars. Some platforms will combine investors into a Special Purpose Vehicle, which will result in only a single entity on a company's cap table.

In addition to the general Reg CF or Reg D platforms, there are numerous other industry-specific platforms (like Harvest Returns) that may be more appropriate for your specific product or company.

An important consideration is the fees charged by the crowdfunding platform and how those fees will impact your company's cost of capital. Some platforms have no upfront fees but require companies to put together their own legal documents (which can quickly become very expensive). Others take a commissioned-based fee. Average upfront fees as a percentage of proceeds range between 6 percent and 10 percent for Regulation D offerings. Still others have ala carte fees schedules for marketing services or legal document preparation. A general rule of thumb is that the more funds a company raises, the lower their cost of capital will be, and vice versa.

2. **Create a Compelling Campaign:** Your campaign should be engaging, informative, and visually appealing. Use high-quality images and videos to showcase your invention/product and explain how it works. Everyone likes a good story, so make sure your campaign tells one, whether that is how you came to create your product, or the impact it is having on customers. Be sure to include a clear call-to-action and a sense of urgency to encourage backers to support your campaign. According to statistics cited by Zippia, crowdfunding campaigns with personal videos raised 150 percent more than those campaigns done without videos.[4] This statistic matches our experience at Harvest Returns, with those campaigns with videos that show a family farmer or rancher working on their operation adding a sense of community and tangibility to the offering.

   Each crowdfunding campaign will be marketed differently to potential investors, based on several factors determined by offering solicitation restrictions, offering type, and crowdfunding platform specifics. Harvest Returns hosts a webinar for most of our offerings, with the entrepreneur giving his or her "pitch" to a live audience and taking investor questions. We also use email campaigns extensively to our pool of investors that

4. Kaitlin Mazur, *25 Critical Crowdfunding Statistics [2023]: How Many Crowdfunding Platforms Are There*, ZIPPIA.COM (Nov. 3, 2022), www.zippia.com/advice/crowdfunding-statistics/.

are specifically interested in these kinds of offerings. Because they are allowed to do open solicitation, Reg CF portals will often market their company's offerings with press releases, paid social media posts, or search advertisements. Sometimes these marketing services are built into a platform's offering fees, while other times they are optional.

3. **Set Realistic Funding Goals:** Determine how much money you need to raise to bring your invention/product to market and set a funding goal that makes sense. Be sure to factor in all costs associated with production, marketing, and shipping. Keep in mind that investors generally don't like to commit money to things that appear self-serving, like a high founder salary on a pre-revenue startup or for repayment of a loan to founders. Though some reasonable operating expenses are expected, most investors want their money to go toward growing the business so they can get repaid. If you are fortunate to enjoy a wildly successful campaign that reaches or exceeds its maximum funding goal, then you will likely have plenty of money to put toward sales and marketing of your product. But if your raise barely squeaks past its minimum funding target, you are going to have to prioritize uses of funds toward where they will make the most impact. Be sure to have contingency for how you will deploy the capital at hand if it turns out to be much less than you expected to raise.

   Sophisticated or accredited investors in Reg D campaigns are going to pay close attention to your company's valuation. They do not want to invest in companies that have unrealistic expectations of value that could result in a loss of some or all of their capital due to future dilution or "down rounds" from subsequent funding raises.

   Because it can be very difficult for early stage or pre-revenue companies to place a realistic valuation on their businesses, some platforms allow for investments in convertible or SAFE (Simple Agreement for Future Equity) notes. These agreements come in several forms, but usually involve the right to convert an investment into a company's stock in the future. Convertible notes might require a company to pay interest to investors on a regular basis or to defer it until maturity or an equity conversion. Still other platforms offer revenue sharing or royalty agreements, allowing investors to receive money directly from the sales of a company's products until the investment is repaid.

4. **Offer Attractive Rewards:** Backers may be more likely to support your campaign if they receive something tangible in return. This is especially true of campaigns on social funding sites. Offer rewards that are relevant to your invention/product and that backers will find valuable. Examples include early access to the product, exclusive merchandise, and personalized thank-you notes. If you operate a manufacturing or production facility, consider offering personal visits. Many Harvest Returns investors decided they would like to inspect the farm or ranch before investing, so we often

help coordinate those visits with our fundraising sponsors. Finally, some platforms will encourage you to offer bonus shares to encourage higher or early commitments.

5. **Promote Your Campaign:** Once your campaign is live, promote it through social media, email marketing, and other channels. Encourage your friends, family, and colleagues to share your campaign with their networks as well. Note: check with the crowdfunding platform to make sure you are in compliance with rules on solicitation to potential investors. Be sure to have a discussion with your crowdfunding platform on whether they expect you to do most of the promotion, or if the platform offers those services.

   If you are promoting your own raise, know your target audience. Zippia statistics say that the average age range of crowdfunding backers is between 24 and 35. Because people generally increase in wealth with age, Regulation D campaigns with higher investment minimums, such as those of $10,000 and up, are likely to appeal to older, wealthier investors. If using social media or advertising, make sure you target the posts and ads to the right demographic. Additionally, if your product or invention falls into a niche category, and you are allowed to openly solicit, then consider targeted advertising on places where people who are likely to use that product gather online. Discussion sites like Reddit or Facebook Groups or the streaming service YouTube allow for hyper-focused ad targeting. Digital marketing can be complex and targeting algorithms frequently change, so seek expert advice if you need it. Though the technology is older, email newsletters have grown in popularity recently and are another potential marketing avenue for your campaign.

6. **Engage with Your Backers:** Respond to comments and questions from your backers in a timely and professional manner. Keep them updated on the progress of your campaign, any new major sales or other news, and show your appreciation for their support. Also per Zippia data, crowdfunding campaigns with regular updates raise 126 percent more than the campaigns with no updates.

By following these steps, a crowdfunding campaign will be doubly successful in marketing your invention and product and generating the funds to bring it to the masses. Know that this strategy will work better for some companies than others. A business to consumer (B2C) company that is actively trying to build an audience for its products is going to get more potential customers out of a crowdfunding campaign than one that focuses on marketing to other businesses. Similarly, some niche platforms, like ours at Harvest Returns, are geared toward higher net worth investors who often invest to support specific types of companies, such as regenerative agriculture.

KEEPING MOMENTUM AFTER THE RAISE

Once your successful crowdfunding campaign is over it's imperative that your company make the most of the funds you've raised. An example of this momentum can be found with one of Harvest Returns' successful farming companies. Established in 2019, Wild Oasis Bison Ranch is a woman-owned and family-operated ranch. The company raises their majestic bison on the beautiful grasslands of Montana with minimal human intervention in a natural environment, without hormones, antibiotics, or pesticides. In 2023, they decided to expand their operation using a debt crowdfunding campaign with Harvest Returns and raised nearly a half million dollars. In addition to expanding their bison herd, Wild Oasis put a significant portion of their funds raised toward product development and marketing. The company's CEO Lori Moore said, "We've started an additional website to promote our jerky, launched subscription boxes, gift boxes, and limited time flavors, while being highly interactive with our customers. We've also hired an e-commerce coach to help us grow exponentially." Though these marketing strategies will take time to produce new sales, Lori has already noticed an increase in her company's revenue following the campaign.

Some crowdfunding platforms will even continue to help companies with successful raises grow their sales. At Harvest Returns, we love to talk about our portfolio companies in our blog, email newsletters, and social media posts. We often link directly to their online store pages to help them convert new customers.

PittMoss continued to see business growth long after their raises on the Harvest Returns platform were completed. According to their CEO Brian Scott, they had a "really great referral from a dog breeder that invested in us on Harvest Returns and uses our animal bedding products for his puppies," which resulted in a new recurring commercial sale. Also a very respected organic grower saw the company on Harvest Returns and has been using PittMoss products.

Though it can be difficult to accurately measure the impact of a crowdfunding campaign on increased sales, most companies see at least some increase in revenue directly attributable to their campaigns.

PittMoss' Brian Scott said, "anecdotally, we have a lot of people writing back to us (e-mail on our website) about how much they liked the product and the names of some of their local stores for us to reach out to from a sales perspective. If I had to guess, I would say that we picked up 20–30 new garden centers from these sorts of activities. So these would be spin out B2B sales and not just B2C sales—but a number of sales leads have come out of these campaigns."

Not only can crowdfunding campaigns bring your company funding and product exposure, but they can also gain the attention of future potential investors.

We get a lot more investor interest from these types of campaigns—either from individuals, angel groups, investment banks, or even some venture capital firms. It's safe to say that plenty of larger investors are following these sites to look for good opportunities to invest in some early-stage companies that might be under the radar. We have had at least two substantial investor groups that reached out to us and later invested as a result of them finding us on one of the CF platforms. A local Chicago Angel Group heard about us through a third party that invested through Harvest Returns and I think over time, they have invested about $500k in the company.

Crowdfunding platforms often have many thousands or even millions of registered investors, so even a campaign that fizzles from a fundraising standpoint can help expose a new product to a large audience and increase sales—and drive feedback that will help improve your business. A deliberate approach to planning and bringing on expert advice will increase the chances of a successful crowdfunding campaign.

Chapter 4

How to Market Your Invention or Company to Investors and Accelerators

Andrew D. Ive

Thanks for coming along to this chapter on how to market your invention to investors and accelerators. Investors and accelerators do not usually invest in an invention alone. Typically, they see the invention as the beginning of a company, a startup. Given that, this chapter should really be called "How to market your invention / startup to investors and accelerators."

WHY ME?

I was asked to write this chapter for a few reasons. Most importantly, I have been in your position. I've spent a lot of my working life as an entrepreneur. I've invented a product, protected it, raised money from investors, and launched it to market. In short, I've been on the inventor side of the table.

I started a venture capital company called Big Idea Ventures, also known as BIV. Over the last five years or so my team and I have become the most active investors in food technology globally today. We have a global network of accelerators in New York, Paris, and Singapore. We have invested in over 100 companies in more than 30 countries.

I have also been an investor and led accelerators, supporting inventors, entrepreneurs, and scientists from around the world.

So if you're searching for some suggestions on how to market your invention to investors or accelerators, I hope you will think that perhaps you've come to the right place.

If you're reading this chapter, you are probably an inventor and want to get funding from investors or accelerators. So let's go get some money, shall we?

THE FIRST AND MOST IMPORTANT QUESTION

I have a question for you, or to be clearer, I have a question you should be asking yourself. Why are you doing it? There are many different reasons why you might want to market your invention to an investor or an accelerator. Your "why" is the most important question you will ask yourself when it comes to finding the right investor or accelerator for your likelihood of success and certainly for your mental health.

Let me explain.

CHEMISTRY IS EVERYTHING

You need to find your investor match.

If you are doing this for the money, then you need to be looking for investors who have the same motivation. If you are doing this to make the world a better place, for goodness's sake, look for investors who have the same motivations. Are there other motivations than making large stacks of money or healing the world? Sure there are.

Some founders are driven to build empires, some are doing it to see their invention in the world, some just do it to enjoy the journey and have fun. What is your own why?

OK—have you figured it out? I'm guessing it's actually pretty easy. You know exactly why you want to get investors, right?

Now you have figured out your why, you should be out there looking for investors who have the same "why." Or at least damn close. If you prioritize money and accept an investment from someone who values altruism, it will likely lead to a difficult, unpleasant, and possibly short experience for everyone involved.

Let's go a little deeper on the investor match approach.

If you have an invention that you have not yet begun bringing to market, then you are at what's called the pre-seed or seed stage.

Why do I call that point out? Because investors come in all shapes and sizes. Some investors are focused on seed stage investments, others are focused on more mature companies. Some investors are focused on companies in a specific sector—food, biotech, software, cybersecurity, AI, and so on.

As you are a seed stage company, you only want to spend your precious time on investors who write checks to companies at the seed stage. Perhaps there's a small part of your brain that is right now saying "Hold up, why can't I talk to all investors? Maybe an investor who usually invests in established companies will find my invention so appealing that they decide to fund it?"

Been there, done that. I've wasted so many hours, days, and weeks chasing the wrong investors.

This is your rodeo. You can ignore everything on these pages, do your own thing, go crazy, maybe it will even work out. Crazier things have happened. But one thing I want you to always remember, money is the oxygen your company needs. Don't ever run out of oxygen. Bad idea.

You might be lucky with an investor who doesn't usually invest in seed stage companies. Sure, have a coffee with them, what's the worst thing that can happen except a caffeine headache. But you need to be as efficient as possible; time is your enemy. When those big consumer goods companies market their products to people, they know exactly who they are trying to attract. They have their target audience so dialed in even though they could afford to market to absolutely everyone. Why can they afford that? Because they've been efficient in how they market their products. Your product is your invention; your goal is to find investors who invest in inventions. Simple, but not easy.

ONE MORE TIME

There are investors who are focused on writing checks to people with inventions. Good news! You don't need to talk to all investors. Just focus on those who invest in inventors or founders at your stage. Your target audience just dramatically shrunk—don't worry, that's a good thing. When developing your invention, the main goal is to save time to reach the right investors quickly, which increases your chances of survival and success in the long run.

At the pre-seed or seed stage, there are a few types of investors who write checks. Let's dig in.

WHO ARE TYPICAL SEED INVESTORS?

Seed investors include the following:

- **Friends, Family, and Fools:** This is often the first place that inventors or entrepreneurs will go to look for investors. It's exactly as it sounds, friends and family who believe in you and your invention enough so they are prepared to write you a check. A few suggestions—if you decide to let a friend or family invest in your invention, be clear about your goals and create a legal agreement that outlines the terms of their investment. Having it clearly laid out, legal, and agreed will make family or friends events in the future a lot easier. Make it official, so they don't have to keep bringing it up EVERY time they see you. :)
- **Angel Investors:** Wealthy individuals who provide capital for a startup, usually in exchange for convertible debt or more recently SAFEs (Simple Agreements for Future Equity). Angel investors can be found in your town or city. They can be wealthy people associated with your church, local chamber of commerce, and other similar organizations.
- **Accelerators:** Organizations designed to accelerate the growth and success of startups by giving them a range of support. In some cases that support includes money, mentorship, access to a relevant network of potential partners, investors, collaborators, and more. In our case, we've built a global network of teams who find, invest, and support young companies throughout the world. Our goal is to work with them to help them scale to global success. Our mission is to solve the world's greatest challenges by supporting the inventors, entrepreneurs, scientists, and engineers with the big ideas.

- **Venture Capital Firms:** Professional investors who manage funds to invest in early-stage companies with high growth potential in exchange for equity. Worth mentioning, VCs do not usually invest in pre-seed or seed stage companies. That's not in stone but do your due diligence before spending lots of time writing emails, getting warm introductions, or going along to meetings.
- **Seed Venture Capital Funds:** Specialized venture capital funds focused exclusively on seed-stage funding. Yes, there are VC funds who are focused on the pre-seed and seed stage. Google and LinkedIn are your friends. Use them to find companies who are looking for companies of your stage and sector.
- **Crowdfunding Platforms:** Online platforms where individuals can collectively invest in startup ventures in return for equity, rewards, or sometimes product pre-orders. There are many crowdfunding platforms across most of the sectors, and not knowing yours, it's tough for me to point you in the right direction. Again, LinkedIn and Google should be a good start. One recommendation—find someone in your network, if possible, who has gone through the process with the platforms you are considering, find real case studies of success. If you can't, don't waste your time.
- **Corporate Venture Capital Funds:** These are investment funds set up by established companies to invest in new startups, often in related fields or sectors where the corporation wants to expand its presence or innovation. There are corporations out there looking for great innovations. Some have even created teams who have the goal of finding the best inventions and, in some cases, investing and perhaps even investing. There are some "watchouts" when it comes to working with corporates. That discussion would be a few chapters in of itself. The basic idea though is to find corporates who have successfully worked with other startups in the past. Ask to be introduced to other startups who have worked with your potential investor before signing on the dotted line.

Over the last few decades, I've had some great conversations with different entrepreneurs. Those who are starting to raise money for the first time often believe investors are all about the money. They think all investors care about it making much more of it.

The interesting thing is that investors who are investing in inventions, or companies at the pre-seed or seed stage, are often comfortable with the fact that they may never see their money again. The reality of investing this early in a company's life cycle is that most investments will fail. I make this point because if investors were just about the money, most would probably not be investing this early. This is important because if it's not just about the money, there are other key reasons why seed investors are writing those checks.

If you understand why they write those checks, you are that much closer to being able to successfully market your invention to them. In other words, if you go into your meeting talking about how much money they are going to make, and that's not what is motivating them, you are selling something this investor isn't buying.

So what are the main motivations for seed investors to invest?

MOTIVATIONS FOR MAKING SEED INVESTMENTS

Seed investments are made for several reasons, including:

- **High Return Potential:** Okay. This is the "making money" reason that is certainly one reason why seed investors make investments. In my experience, it's "a" reason rather than "the" reason. It's true that early-stage companies can offer significant returns on investment if they grow successfully. Getting in early can mean a lot of financial upside for the investors who come in early and take more of the risks.
- **Innovation and Impact:** Investors may be motivated by the opportunity to be involved in new technologies that can have a meaningful impact on a specific industry or on a mission the investor cares about. Increasingly investors are looking to use some of their money to achieve a positive impact. That's what is meant by impact investing. If your invention makes a positive impact on the world, perhaps as a more sustainable way to achieve a goal, you could be checking a key box for those who want to use their capital to have a positive impact.
- **Influence and Involvement:** Seed investing allows investors to be more involved in the development and strategic direction of the company.
- **Networking and Ecosystem Building:** Being an active seed investor can expand one's network within the startup ecosystem, providing access to further investment opportunities and partnerships. By investing in one or more startups, investors can meet other investors and other investment opportunities and expand their network.
- **Personal Interest or Passion:** Some investors are drawn to startups operating in fields they are personally interested in or passionate about.
- **Supporting Entrepreneurship:** There's a sense of fulfillment in supporting entrepreneurs and contributing to job creation and economic growth.
- **Bragging Rights:** Some investors write checks because they consider it interesting and something they can chat about with their business associates and friends at social occasions. It keeps them in touch with the cutting edge of business, with true innovation.

As you spend time with potential investors, you will begin to understand their motives for chatting with you. It's likely they will fall into one of the preceding reasons.

Why do you care? Because the better you understand why they want to invest, you can determine (1) if you want them as an investor and if you do (2) how to position your invention or opportunity so it aligns more clearly with what the investor is seeking.

Now let's circle back to this chapter's question: **How to successfully market your invention to investors and accelerators.**

The secret of successful marketing is to efficiently talk to the people who want what it is you're selling. You need to deeply understand your ideal investors needs and preferences, and when you find them, you need to ensure you can clearly communicate a compelling proposal that resonates with them.

Successful marketing hinges on taking the right investors through your offer; it's about storytelling that connects emotionally, showcasing how your invention will allow them to meet their investor needs. It requires a mix of creativity, analytical thinking, and a commitment to matching what you are delivering to what your ideal investors deeply want.

MARKETING YOUR INVENTION TO INVESTORS

The storytelling to investors today is done through the pitch deck. A presentation, which gives you the opportunity to take an investor through the key information they usually consider before making an investment decision. Let me take you through a decent framework for a pitch deck.

One of the most important steps is to create a pitch deck that will kick ass. The following outline is what I and others have successfully used in the past.

How to Create a Pitch Deck to Wow Investors

Creating a pitch deck that clearly outlines your opportunity to investors can be covered using the following slides. Here's a structured approach to crafting a compelling pitch deck:

1. Title Slide
    - Company Name: Clearly displayed.
    - Logo: If available.
    - Tagline: A brief, impactful statement about your business.
    - Contact Information: Email or professional social media links.
2. Problem Slide
    - Identify the Problem: Clearly articulate the problem your business intends to solve.
    - Relatability: Make it relatable to ensure the audience understands the importance.

3. Solution Slide
   - Your Solution: Present your product or service as the solution to the identified problem.
   - Unique Value Proposition (UVP): Highlight what makes your solution unique and better than existing alternatives.
4. Market Opportunity Slide
   - Market Size: Quantify the size of the opportunity using TAM (Total Available Market), SAM (Serviceable Available Market), and SOM (Serviceable Obtainable Market).
   - Target Market: Define who your ideal customers are.
   - Growth Projections: Show expected market growth over time.
5. Product or Service Slide
   - Product Description: Detail what you are selling or offering.
   - Product Status: Development stage, beta versions, or availability.
   - Demo: If possible, include a brief demo or screenshots.
6. Business Model Slide
   - Revenue Model: Explain how your business makes money.
   - Pricing Strategy: Detail your pricing model.
   - Sales & Distribution Model: Describe how you plan to sell and distribute your product or service.
7. Traction Slide
   - Proof of Concept: Show any existing traction, pilot users, initial sales, or partnerships.
   - Milestones Reached: Highlight key milestones already achieved.
8. Marketing and Sales Strategy Slide
   - Customer Acquisition: Outline your strategies for acquiring customers.
   - Growth Strategy: Describe how you plan to grow your business.
9. Competition Slide
   - Competitive Landscape: Identify key competitors and alternatives in the market.
   - Differentiation: Clearly state how your solution is different and/or better.
10. Financials Slide
    - Financial Projections: Provide a three- to five-year forecast of key financials, including revenue, profit, and cash flow.

- Current Financial Status: If applicable, include current revenue, burn rate, and runway.

11. Team Slide
    - Key Team Members: Introduce your team, highlighting relevant experience and roles.
    - Advisors: Mention any notable advisors or mentors.
12. Ask Slide
    - Funding Requirement: Specify how much funding you are seeking.
    - Use of Funds: Outline how the investment will be used.

Tips for a Successful Pitch Deck

- **Keep It Concise:** Ideally, limit your pitch deck to around 10–14 slides.
- **Engaging Design:** Use high-quality graphics and avoid clutter. Each slide should be visually compelling but not distract from the message.
- **Tell a Story:** Weave your slides into a narrative that captures the essence of your business and why it matters.
- **Practice Your Pitch:** Be ready to confidently present your deck and answer any questions investors might have.

Remember, the goal of your pitch deck is not only to secure funding but to get the next meeting. Your goal for the next meeting is to be invited to the next meeting. Until you get to due diligence and the potential for a real deal.

BTW, at Big Idea Ventures we usually advise our accelerator companies to create two pitch decks. One to present during a meeting or pitch session. This deck will have few words, bold, emotional graphics, and photos that compel and make the point for each slide. And a pitch deck, with far more words, that you can send after the first meeting, which can do the heavy lifting of communication, without you needing to explain anything. The typed words do all the work in what I call your "leave behind" or "send after" deck.

A few additional tips to consider when "pitching" to an investor.

You aren't more likely to get money the more you talk. When you walk into an investor meeting, try to spend the first 15 or 20 minutes asking your investor questions. It may seem like cheating, but you can actually ask an investor what they are interested in, why they are an investor, what they find exciting about being an investor, what kinds of investments they are looking for. What's also mind-blowing is that investors will often tell you. Why? Because they want to see if what you have fits what they are seeking.

Mind blown, but this is a two-way street. Investors are *looking* for certain types of investments. They want to find them. They want to write those checks.

And there are almost definitely investors out there who are looking for exactly what you have. You just have to find them.

So when you sit down with an investor, don't be shy about asking them about themselves, their goals, what types of investments they are actively looking for and then take a breath. After getting the answers to these questions, can your invention meet their goals? Are they motivated by the same "why" as you? If your invention can truly meet their investor needs, and they are motivated by the same "why" as you, this could be your ideal investor.

If they could be, you need to take them through your pitch deck, making sure you clearly hit the points that demonstrate how it meets their needs.

Whew. But it's true. Listening is a key skill for fundraising. Every meeting you have is getting you closer to understanding not only the investors you're meeting but also the true characteristics of your ideal investor. And believe it or not, as someone who has been married for 25 years, you'll know it when you meet the right one for you.

So we've spent a good amount of time focused on how to market to investors; now let's touch on the accelerators out there.

STARTUP ACCELERATIONS

First, let's tackle what is a startup accelerator?

The Basics

A startup accelerator is a program designed to support early-stage companies, usually pre-seed and seed companies, through mentorship and financing. Startups often enter accelerators for a fixed period of time and as part of a cohort of companies. The process will usually culminate in a pitch event, called a demo day, to introduce the startups to investors.

I was taught how to run an accelerator by one of the first guys at one of the world's best accelerators. I won't embarrass him by mentioning him here (hey Doody), but he really did roll up his sleeves and mentor me through multiple cohorts. Helping me understand how to work with very early-stage companies and do everything possible to help them to become successful. I love entrepreneurs. They are the magic of the business world. Everything you see around you right now was created once upon a time by an inventor, an entrepreneur. They literally change the world and, hopefully, will continue to do so for decades to come.

Big Idea Ventures, the company I started, is centered on inventors—entrepreneurs, scientists, and engineers. We believe we need to find the best of them, tackling the world's biggest challenges, and do everything we can to make them successful. It will get us out of many of the messes we've got ourselves into.

Our accelerators are a key part of what we do to support the entrepreneurs we invest in. We now have teams in North America, Asia, and Europe, which gives us global coverage, finding and supporting teams in many countries. And we expect to build more ecosystems in key places around the world to give greater support to amazing entrepreneurs. We're focused on food and agriculture right now as these sectors are critical for climate change, global warming, and living for an extended period of time on this incredible planet. One day I can see Big Idea Ventures working to support entrepreneurs in other sectors—biotechnology, health, therapeutics, and more.

Please be aware that not all accelerators are equal. There is not some government course or certification to run a good accelerator. It's a shame because if you waste your time with a team who can't actually help and add much value, it could impact your company's likelihood of success. A good accelerator will help you understand your gaps and do what they can to help you fill them. They'll do this through their own team and their network of advisors, mentors, partners, investors, government and academic relationships, and more. Accelerators worth your time will provide access to investors, mentors, other startups, government contacts, academics (if necessary), and more. They'll help you find the resources to help you grow and succeed.

Warning!

Please be careful that you have done your due diligence to ensure the accelerator is worth your time. Go talk to some of their previous companies to understand just how good (or not) they are. Remember—anyone can call themselves an accelerator—make sure you know what you are getting when you join one. Some corporations create their own accelerators. More often than not, they're not great unless they are run by people who have started and grown companies like yours. I was an entrepreneur three times over before I worked on my first accelerator. Corporates know how to run big companies with lots of resources and at a size your company may never achieve in your lifetime. Unless the corporate accelerator is run by someone who has been where you sit, they probably can't help you with the challenges a company of your size will face. Sure they probably have a great brand, but should they be advising you on how to solve your challenges?

Perhaps the best way to explain how to market your invention to accelerators, I'll take you through how to apply to ours, at Big Idea Ventures. The great thing about accelerators is they are easily found. They have a website, with a form to complete and a timetable for accepting companies into their accelerator.

What you need to do is to ensure you are applying to the right accelerator for you and then follow the process. So get a description of the accelerators you are considering and ensure they check your boxes.

For example—let me take you through Big Idea Ventures . . .

Big Idea Ventures (BIV) is a venture capital firm that primarily focuses on investing in and accelerating startups in the **food technology sector**, particularly those working on **alternative proteins**, **alternative fats**, **ingredients** and

sustainable food solutions, and **innovative food technologies**. Their mission often involves supporting companies that aim to address global challenges such as food security, sustainability, and the environmental impact of food production. Big Idea Ventures runs accelerator programs to nurture startups by providing them with funding, mentorship, and access to networks of industry experts and potential partners. The firm typically invests in early-stage companies around the world, aiming to foster innovation in the food industry for a healthier and more sustainable future.

I've highlighted a few keywords because if your invention does not fit into one of these areas—we are 100 percent irrelevant to you. Even so, I can't tell you how many emails I get every day from inventors and entrepreneurs who are pitching me on sectors outside my focus. It's a complete waste of my time and theirs.

Perhaps the most important thing you can do when marketing to investors and accelerators is just make sure you are marketing to people who actually can and do invest in your sector. This is not so much a numbers game that if you send 100 emails to 100 of the wrong investors you'll get an investor. Better to send ten emails to investors who care about what you do.

Now you have filtered down your accelerator list—it's time to apply.

Our acceleration application process is quite similar to many others:

To get into the Big Idea Ventures (BIV) accelerator, follow these general steps:

1. **Understand BIV Focus Areas:** Big Idea Ventures focuses on startups in the alternative protein sector, sustainable food technology, and innovations that can significantly impact the food industry. Ensure your startup aligns with their investment thesis.
2. **Prepare Your Application:**
    - Pitch Deck: Create a compelling and concise presentation that covers your business model, team, market analysis, financial projections, and how the investment will be used.
    - Prototype or MVP (Minimum Viable Product): If applicable, having a prototype or MVP can significantly strengthen your application by demonstrating your commitment and the feasibility of your product.
3. **Apply Online:** Visit our website and navigate to their application page. We have specific application periods for their accelerator programs, so ensure you're applying within the open window.
4. **Networking:** Engaging with the BIV community or attending industry events where BIV representatives might be present can provide valuable networking opportunities. A referral or direct introduction can make a difference.
5. **Prepare for Interviews:** If your application is shortlisted, you'll likely be invited for interviews. Be ready to discuss your business in detail,

including technical aspects, market strategy, and financials. Demonstrating passion, knowledge, and the potential for impact will be crucial.

6. **Feedback and Iteration:** Whether successful or not in your initial application, seek feedback. Use any insights gained to refine your proposition or approach for future applications if necessary.

Remember, each accelerator has its unique selection criteria and process. It's essential to tailor your application to meet the accelerator's specific requirements and demonstrate how your invention / startup aligns with their missions.

If I had to take all of the preceding and simplify it into just a few sentences, the basics are—don't waste your precious time on "all" investors, focus on finding your ideal investors, and be really clear why you and they should be going on the same journey together. Be vigilant about who you take money from because an investor relationship can last years and sometimes decades. If you don't want to spend time with these investors, if they aren't people you would enjoy spending time with, don't take their money.

I hope this chapter is incredibly useful to you. If you use it to create something amazing and make a contribution, then writing it was worth my time and learning it was worth yours.

If you would like to reach out and tell me your story, come find me at BigIdeaVentures.com or on LinkedIn. Good luck, go get your ideal investors, I'm cheering you on.

Chapter 5
Leveraging Real-World Successes

Emily Kenison

INTRODUCTION

Success doesn't always come from having deep pockets; it often comes from a combination of resourcefulness, resilience, and strategic decision-making. Throughout my entrepreneurial journey, I've had to make every dollar count. Starting with limited resources, I grew the business into a multimillion-dollar brand and selling in major retailers like Target. My experiences show that it is possible to launch, scale, and achieve market success without relying on heavy investments or elaborate budgets.

This chapter focuses on practical strategies and lessons learned that any entrepreneur can apply to bring their invention to market, build a brand, and leverage media attention—even with limited funds. From customer-centric approaches and bootstrapped marketing to navigating the challenges of counterfeits, I will share actionable steps to grow your invention on a lean budget. Whether you're just starting out or looking for ways to maximize your impact, the principles outlined here will guide you through leveraging real-world success with the resources you have at hand.

BOOTSTRAPPING INNOVATION: A JOURNEY FROM INVENTING TO SCALING

As a lawyer turned inventor, my road to entrepreneurship initially started when I stumbled in the office at my first law firm job. It was in that moment that my first invention Straplets—shoe accessories that instantly transform the look of your shoes while adding comfort and support—was sparked. Since then, I have led my second invention RobeCurls to win seven product innovation awards and created an entirely new category of heatless hair tools on the market. I started with only $500 to invest in RobeCurls, which has now amassed $4 million in sales and continues to receive 5-star reviews from customers, paving the way for a new category in haircare. I have since gone on to found Emikeni Inc., the parent company behind the brands we bring to life, founded with the mission to empower women-led entrepreneurship for the future of invention.

From the beginning, my focus was on empowering my customers to have simpler routines that benefited their every day. Before RobeCurls, I was damaging my hair every morning with a curling iron to the point it was brittle. When the viral TikTok trend #robecurls came to my attention, I started my journey to find the perfect heatless hair product. Turns out I had to invent it to find the perfect product that would change the course of history for hairstyling products. Bootstrapping my invention was no easy task, but there are organic methods you can use to leverage your invention for real-world success.

Bootstrapping is defined as "to get (oneself or something) into or out of a situation using existing resources." Leveraging what I had already learned with Straplets initiated the ability to bootstrap RobeCurls into existence. I operated with a limited budget for marketing because every dollar made was put back into inventory. There are a few ways I was able to manage marketing RobeCurls on a lean budget that elevated my brand to reach new customers and create meaningful connections in the industry.

CUSTOMER-CENTRIC APPROACH TO EDUCATE CUSTOMERS

One of the early marketing strategies we implemented was to have a customer-centric approach. A customer-centric approach focuses on delivering the best experience possible to customers. One way I approached this was to implement one-on-one CurlTalks, which are virtual curl classes that every customer can participate in. Through an easy Calendly link, customers are able to book a 15-minute time slot to learn how to use RobeCurls more effectively. This gave the opportunity for customers to experiment in finding the right type of curl they were looking for with personal instructions. Each call I talk through how to properly set up their hair to get the best curls, as well as implement feedback as they wrap their hair around the curling headband. Implementing this customer-centric approach early on allowed for me to connect with customers and create a personal connection. In turn, it inspired customers to become brand advocates, as well as provided valuable feedback for me to refine how I created tutorials for a variety of hair types.

Building Connection with Customers

Building a connection with customers is vital for market success. To start building a connection, I focused on the customer experience first. Building a positive customer journey opened up the capacity for a strong online community for my brands. One of the ways to uphold the integrity of a positive connection is to hire a person specific to the Customer Delight stage of the process. Placing someone in the role who enjoys connecting with customers, helping them find the right product, and managing any issues gives the ability to have better reviews and positive customer feedback. Unlike other competitors on the market, we focused on the customer journey first and built a brand with active communication that supported our customers in return for their purchase. Dedicated customer communication channels including utilizing chat bots, actively responding on social media, and replying to customer emails helps us stay ahead of potential issues and allows customers to voice their needs.

Receiving Reviews and Feedback

Reviews and customer feedback are an important aspect to your brand being seen and how it is received by customers. When RobeCurls was having issues with counterfeits being sent to customers, we managed to catch this issue when customers were reporting that the incorrect product arrived at their address. We immediately sent the right product to remedy the situation, despite not receiving the sales. The direct feedback helped us manage the problem, as well as create a stronger bond with our customers who recognized that we had their best interest in mind. When we received positive reviews, we highlighted the feedback on our social media channels to further share with our community in our dedication to their experience as a customer. Highlighting reviews also caught the attention of publications, which opened up doorways to be featured in top publications with over 3,000 5-star reviews. Customers today focus on reviews before making a purchase, which is why it is important to have a system in place to monitor reviews and respond to feedback.

BUILDING AN AUTHENTIC PERSONAL BRAND (NAVIGATING CHALLENGES AND SETBACKS)

Building an authentic personal brand is not without its challenges and setbacks. Managing and scaling marketing efforts across various platforms pushed us to be adaptable to the changing market landscape. For example, when customers were receiving counterfeits, we had to persist in finding a solution until we could get the knockoffs off the platform. Through the process we listened to and validated customer concerns before offering solutions. While navigating the issue with knockoffs, we also created videos on social media to educate about the issues of ordering through certain platforms and what customers needed to check before making a purchase. As a result, our brand transparency helped us develop a level of trust with customers who were hesitant to make a purchase after having issues with online orders.

Scaling Marketing Efforts

Scaling marketing efforts takes a strategic look at what channels and resources you have available to you. With my brands, we took a three-stage approach to assist the flow of content and customer interaction.

The first stage is the customer being a stranger. The goal in the initial stage is to offer the customer value through education, inspiration, and entertainment with the goal to earn a customer's attention, not force it. To attract customers in this way, we developed meaningful and compelling content that eliminated the barrier to access for understanding what inventions we offered. Actions to initiate this stage of the process included influencer marketing, SEO strategies, engaging landing pages, social media campaigns, paid advertisements when needed, customer reviews, and press coverage. We monitored this through metrics that tracked location, channels, devices, email open rates and clicks, page views, and impressions and engagement on social media.

Part of the success in the first stage is to deliver content that connects with the customer in a way that is authentically your brand. For RobeCurls, I highlighted user-generated content of customers curling their hair, as well as created tutorials and introductions to the product itself. In terms of paid advertisements, we utilized Amazon advertisements to show up as the preferred product listing that in turn got us more views than organically trying to grow through the platform. Instead of setting up social media advertisements on Instagram and TikTok, we chose to organically grow the brand by connecting with influencers and posted regular content on our channels to connect with potential customers.

The second customer stage is the customer being a visitor, which includes fans and followers. The goal of this second stage is to add value and build trust by adapting content to meet customer ambitions and their desire for a solution that your brand provides. We purposefully keep our doors open to welcome customer interest and relationships, instead of just focusing on closing the deal. During this stage, we enable customers to engage with us by providing insightful educational material that shares about the use of our inventions. The actions we take to engage customers is through blogs, newsletters, a live chat bot, customer reviews, contact capability, and utilizing long-tail keywords. The metrics we implemented to track this include monitoring bounce rate, pay per view, time on site, time on page, new versus returning customers, referral traffic, email subscriber growth, email unsubscribes, and email forwards. By implementing educational videos, blogs, and newsletters, it gives us the opportunity for customers to learn in a way that meets them where they are. Each of my brands has its own email system that serves as a way to connect with customers about updates, share educational videos, and highlight positive reviews. Blogs can often coincide with the newsletters, as well as be an extension of any videos we post on social media channels such as YouTube, TikTok, and Instagram.

The final customer stage is the customer choosing to purchase a product and thus becoming a dedicated customer. This stage is referred to as delight, where the customer's success is tangible and builds a positive relationship with our brands. By creating an engaging customer experience, we are able to empower the customer to purchase the solution we have, which in turn creates an advocate for our company. In this stage, we created CurlTalks, manageable return policies, free shipping and other shipping options, high-quality customer support, recognizing and featuring successes through social media, and reward programs. The metrics we monitor to track this are goal conversion rate, sales transactions, time to purchase, assisted conversions, lead capture forms, as well as blog and email subscriptions.

CurlTalks have been the most beneficial aspect of the final customer stage for RobeCurls. Not only did it show who our customers actually were, it also gave us an opportunity to share more about how to use the product for best results. CurlTalks opened up the ability to personally connect and deliver high-quality customer support even after a customer has made a purchase. This approach developed a customer connection that created advocates for our brand, which helped support us through issues with counterfeit sellers. Featuring successes is also a regular part of our social media strategy. On all social media channels, we highlight CurlTalks, reviews, and share user-generated content from customers who have shared about their experience with our brand. This approach helped generate buzz around RobeCurls and made it stand out from competitors.

Omnichannel Presence

One of the aspects we decided on early was to have an omnichannel presence (Figure 5.1). This meant having content flow through to all channels to minimize the effort needed to create something different for each individual channel. We focused on key calendar dates, such as major holidays, as well as certain themes we wanted the brand to focus on. From there, we created YouTube videos that could be turned into blogs and YouTube Shorts. Blogs could then be utilized for newsletters, press releases, and tweets (now referred to as posts on X), while YouTube shorts could become TikTok videos, Reels, LinkedIn posts, and Amazon videos. An omnichannel presence allowed us to use the small resources we had to build a strategy that worked with a small team. By developing videos and creating a plan on Notion, a software designed for organization, it helped us reach more customers without having to create an overwhelming amount of content. This strategy also ensured we had higher-quality content instead of settling for content that did not serve our community in the best way.

Mixing the types of media you create has the ability to reach customers exactly where they are and learn how they interact with content. For some customers, they may resonate more with an educational newsletter and a background of how an invention came to be. While other customers may only interact with social media content and be more focused on engaging with video content. Developing an omnichannel presence meets both of these types of customers and engages them in a way that develops trust over time.

One of the strategies we implemented was sharing educational content about past women inventors. With a theme in place, we created a newsletter that then became a blog and social media content. While the flow of content was slightly different with this approach, it meant that the different channels could be interchangeable for how best to present the content. In the case of the women inventors, the content was created to connect with people who were interested in Emikeni inventions and might be curious about how past inventions help

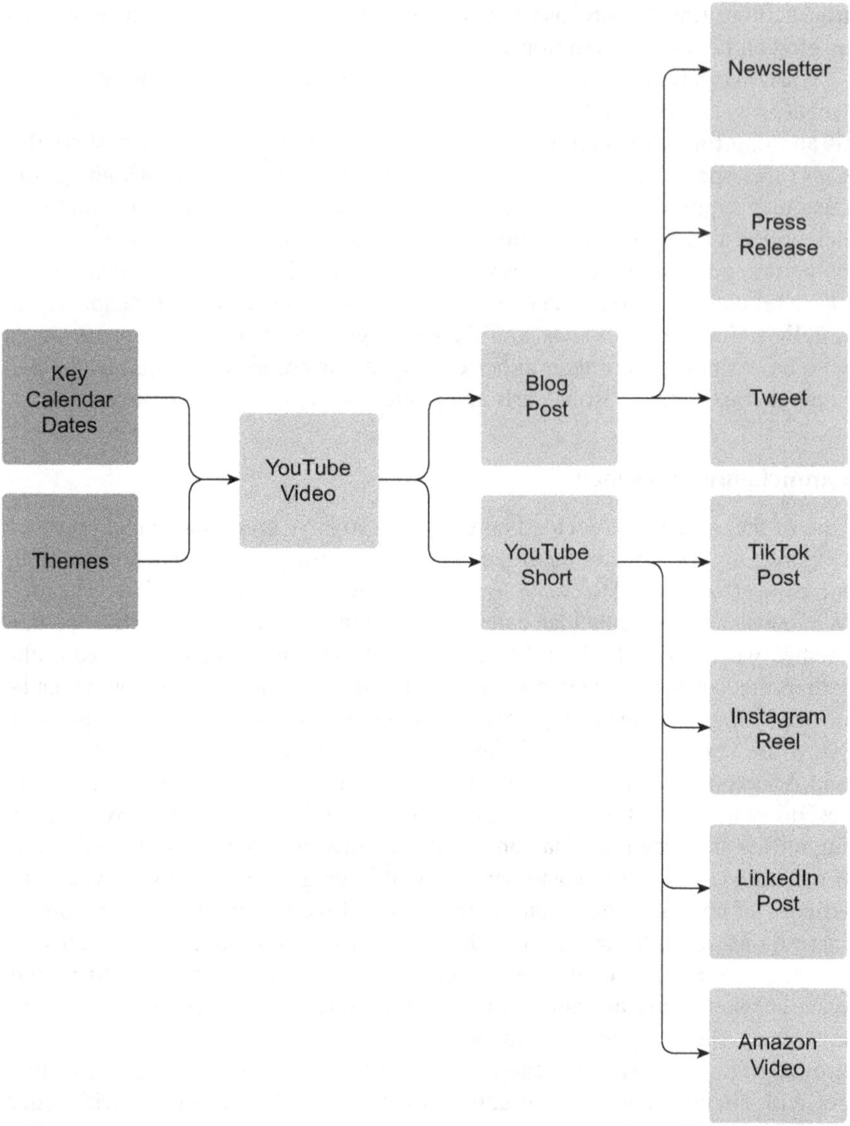

Figure 5.1

modern women inventors today be seen and understood. Developing this unique approach resonated with other women inventors who may not have heard of the historical context of inventions, as well as showcased how important women's ideas are when marketing inventions and receiving funding.

Overall, an omnichannel presence should focus back on the customer journey. Does the content inform how to use the invention? Does it showcase the importance of the customer experience? Is your content flow manageable for the team you have? These are all important questions to ask when developing an omnichannel presence that can support the marketing of your invention.

Challenge of Counterfeits

One of the most challenging aspects of creating an invention is the issue of counterfeits. RobeCurls was amongst the most counterfeited products in 2022. Not only was this heartbreaking to experience as an inventor, but it also stole sales and created customer dissatisfaction with heatless hair tools. Before inventing RobeCurls, I tried every heatless hair tool on the market, which meant I understood the customer frustration with counterfeits coming to their door instead of this revolutionary heatless hair tool that was promised. To counteract this issue, we hired a brand protection agency to take down counterfeit sellers. However, when the number of sellers online was reaching in the realm of thousands, this was not enough to combat the issue. What ultimately helped us take hold of the sheer scale and velocity of counterfeit products was using "Schedule A" lawsuits.

Schedule A lawsuits, often filed against multiple defendants in a single action, allowed us to target a large number of counterfeiters quickly and efficiently. By leveraging Schedule A lawsuits, we were able to secure injunctions against counterfeit sellers across multiple platforms. This legal strategy enabled us to shut down fraudulent listings, freeze assets, and enforce our intellectual property rights at scale, giving us the ability to take swift action against the overwhelming presence of counterfeit products. This approach, combined with our robust IP protection, was instrumental in protecting our brand, ensuring that our customers were purchasing the authentic RobeCurls product, and preserving the trust we had worked so hard to build.

Counterfeits are an issue for inventions and can show up faster than you might initially realize, and on a scale that you never imagined. It is important to protect your inventions and brand early on to counteract this issue. By having the online presence early and implementing protections against counterfeit sellers, it can help show that your product is the authentic one on the market.

The Importance of Intellectual Property Protection

Protecting your invention through intellectual property (IP) rights is one of the most critical steps an inventor can take to safeguard against counterfeits and build long-term value. For RobeCurls, securing patents, trademarks, and copyrights was essential in creating a legal foundation to protect my invention from imitation and unauthorized use. The IP protection we established not only gave us a way to legally pursue counterfeit sellers, but it also created a layer of trust for our customers. By clearly communicating that RobeCurls is a patented product, we reassured customers that they were purchasing a legitimate, innovative solution, which further built the brand's credibility in the market.

Moreover, having robust IP protections in place helped me navigate legal challenges quickly and effectively. With patents securing the product's unique design and function, and trademarks safeguarding the brand's identity, we were able to actively fight back against knockoffs that attempted to deceive customers and erode trust. The IP protection allowed us to hire a brand protection agency to remove counterfeit products from online platforms and protect future innovations as we expanded our product line.

The value provided by IP protection goes beyond just deterring counterfeits; it also becomes a key asset for your company. Investors and partners often view strong IP protection as a sign of a secure, scalable, and innovative business, which can positively impact funding opportunities and retail expansion. RobeCurls, backed by patents and trademarks, was better positioned to negotiate partnerships with major retailers like Target, who appreciated the integrity and security that comes with a well-protected product.

Building Trust with Customers

Building an authentic personal brand starts with trust. Trust is built slowly over time with customers online, which is why it is helpful to create content that feels authentic to you and your brand. There is something unique that your brand can bring to the marketplace, and one way of showing that is through sharing your brand story. When writing my brand story I thought about what questions the customer would have when interacting with my inventions. I focused on how the customer would feel reading my story, as well as addressed the pain points that I shared with them. With RobeCurls, I expressed how I had damaged my hair almost to the point of no return with a curling iron. I also educated how the curling iron was made 100 years ago by a man and that there was a huge gap in the market for a heatless hair tool that actually worked. Sharing my frustrations with the hair tool market not only was cathartic but also showed that women are not alone in their struggle to find products that actually serve them and simplify their routines. RobeCurls was a solution to the issue. To further the integrity of the story, I included how RobeCurls holds curls five times longer than other methods and shared the science behind the innovation that could help customers see the value in my invention. All of this information put together in a tangible way for a customer to interact with helped convey my story to the market. As a result, RobeCurls has been featured in top-publications because of the authentic story and personalized branding it brings to the industry.

When thinking of ways to build trust with your customers, look at how you want your brand to be perceived. In my case, I wanted to show the importance of women-led inventions and how there is space for innovation on the market. Customers are looking for inventions that solve problems, and sharing that story helps them find your brand and become a loyal customer.

BUILDING A BRAND ON A BUDGET

I bootstrapped RobeCurls with only $500 in my pocket. It was an incredibly low amount to start with, but it led me to being strategic about what I could do to build a brand. I previously created my first invention Straplets, a stylish detachable shoe accessory, on a budget as well, which gave me the tools I needed to build the branding around RobeCurls much quicker. One of the ways I approached building a brand was to utilize Indiegogo, a platform where we could share our story and raise funds to contribute to the launch of RobeCurls. We reached our goal within 24 hours and doubled it in the first week. Indiegogo and Kickstarter and platforms like them are a great place to start funding your invention.

An additional resource we utilized on a budget was building an online storefront through Shopify. Shopify made it easy to list products and highlight our brand story, as well as take customer orders directly. We also used Amazon, where one in two purchases in the United States is made. To boost our visibility on Amazon, we implemented Amazon advertisements and signed up for Amazon transparency. To manage ads, we connected with good partnerships like Hometown Industries to help position our brand further to show up higher than knockoffs or other competitors in customer searches.

Influencer Partnerships

Influencer partnerships are a great way to build a brand on a budget and can contribute to fast growth. When searching for the right partnership, I looked for influencers who could authentically show what RobeCurls could do and someone who had a big enough reach to make a significant difference for my brand. When I came across Alex Gaboury's YouTube channel I was blown away by her presence and her accessible hair tutorials. She already previously made a video about using a bathrobe belt to curl hair, so it made an easy transition to update the video using RobeCurls. We could not initially afford a regular deal for an influencer partnership, which meant we did a creative profit share approach that worked for both Alex Gaboury and our brand budget. Since uploading the video to YouTube, Alex Gaboury's tutorial on how to use RobeCurls has been seen by over four million people. This is a reach we would not have otherwise been able to achieve on our own. Alex Gaboury is also featured on our shopping channels such as Shopify and Amazon, and on our social media channels where our customers can engage with the tutorial to find out how to achieve curls just like hers.

When looking for influencers to partner with your brand, make sure you are clear in what you can offer and how a creative profit share can be mutually beneficial. Quality content from an important influencer has the ability to reach new market segments that are otherwise harder to reach with just paid advertising or organic content.

Expanding to Retail

Expanding to retail was a huge step forward for my brand and only came two months after launching RobeCurls. Even with a lean budget, we managed to connect with a Diverse Supplier Buyer through Women's Business Enterprise National Council (WBENC) because of being 100 percent woman owned. Walgreens initially accepted RobeCurls into 130 stores and successfully grew the hair care category by 400 percent. Through Walgreens, we were able to show our value in the market, which connected us to partnerships with Urban Outfitters, FabFitFun, and Target.

SCALING WITH EFFECTIVE BOOTSTRAPPED MARKETING STRATEGIES

Scaling with effective bootstrapped marketing strategies is about looking for opportunities that can elevate your brand.

Leveraging Media Opportunities

Without a public relations team, we managed to have coverage of our brands in top publications including *Allure*, *Vogue*, *Glamour*, *Cosmopolitan*, and the *Today Show* with regular mentions. Part of leveraging media opportunity was the method to create press releases, reach out to connections within our network, as well as look for quality leads on platforms that resonated with our brand. We utilized platforms like HARO to receive press coverage and membership with Dreamers & Doers that connected us to media outlets that otherwise would be difficult for a small business to reach. Each time our brands were highlighted in press publications, we would leverage this attention by including it in our newsletters and showcasing the article on social media. We always made sure to highlight and thank the writer who published the article, to ensure they knew how much the press mention meant for our brand.

Collaborations with Brands

Collaborations with brands continue to help us develop a grassroots effort to expand our market reach. Brand collaborations included being a part of the #bamarush campaign with Winky Lux and Bubble Skincare that connected us to Bama coverage across multiple TikTok influencer channels. The brand collaboration created viral content with a unique approach that we could not have created on our own. We further leveraged this content by creating our own video content on YouTube, Instagram, and TikTok and utilized the Bama Rush hashtag to showcase giveaway winners and share more about our inventions. Connecting with like-minded brands like Winky Lux and Bubble Skincare allowed for us to elevate one another's brands and create a meaningful connection in the industry that offered an opportunity for beneficial growth. As a result, our brand name and products appeared in numerous TikTok influencer videos that helped us reach a market that would have been otherwise difficult to connect to.

Applying to Awards

Applying to award competitions can help solidify your brand's authority in the market. Taking this approach helped RobeCurls win seven awards in product innovation that showcased the high-quality design available on the market. Submitting the design details of your invention is one part of award applications, but it also asks for the story of your brand. Navigating how you can tell your brand story in a concise way that shows how important your invention is, as well as communicating the details about the unique design, can help your application stand out amongst hundreds of others that judges receive.

Applying to awards also includes experiences that could solidify funding for your brand. I applied to experiences such as "America's Big Deal" with Joy Mangano (who inspired me to become an inventor) and I even proposed to my fiancé on live television during the competition! It was a memorable experience that gave our brand better visibility and an industry connection. Live television competitions are one award avenue, as well as podcasts that offer the chance for inventors to share their pitch and potentially win funding. We applied for "The Pitch" podcast, which created a unique opportunity to hone our brand's pitch and share with a wider audience about the purpose and mission of the brand. Not every opportunity will lead to funding, but sharing the story of your brand and the importance of your invention to new audiences can expand your market reach.

Power of the Ask

Never underestimate the power of the ask when bootstrapping your invention. My wild story that helped my inventions was when I proposed to Sara Blakely, the inventive mind behind Spanx. In the crowd I held a sign that said "Will you marry me" but had "marry" crossed out with "mentor" written next to it. I have always been inspired by Sara Blakely's inventions, and her visibility as a woman inventor showed that it was possible for me to be an inventor too. I am so lucky she said yes when I proposed to her with Straplets! Since then, she has supported me and my inventions, including helping us get the funding we needed to get inventory for our Target launch.

Sara Blakely's mentorship not only helped me personally as an entrepreneur, but also opened more doors for me when it came to funding and expanding my brand. I am grateful to each person who said yes and gave my brands a chance in the market.

LESSONS LEARNED AND BEST PRACTICES

There are numerous inevitable lessons as an entrepreneur and inventor, but there are a few key factors that can help you find your foundation to leverage real-world success.

Market Your Story

Your brand's story plays an important role in how your invention is received on the market. Showcase how important your invention is to your customers through authentic brand storytelling and educational content that resonates with your target audience. In turn, it helps build authority in your industry and creates opportunities for media coverage that you can further leverage to grow your brand.

Operate with a Lean Budget

You do not need to have a large budget to get into a mass retailer or get press mentions from top publications. Utilizing simple methods of content flow, accessing the resources you already have, and experimenting with marketing strategies can all help build your brand's growth. I started with only $500 and grew my invention's reach to $3 million in revenue with projected growth to $4.5 million. This growth is in direct relation to our efforts to grow the brand in an authentic way that prioritizes the customer journey and delivers a high-quality product that customers love.

Marketing your invention is possible with a bootstrapped budget. With a strategy that works with your current available resources and the ability to showcase the importance of your invention, you can be well on your way to leveraging real-world successes that change industries for the better.

RESOURCES

- HARO: www.helpareporter.com
- Shopify: www.shopify.com
- Dreamers & Doers: www.dreamersdoers.com

Chapter 6
The Power of Radio in Storytelling

Kenya Gipson

In the realm of storytelling, few mediums possess the timeless allure and captivating power of radio. From its humble beginnings to its modern resurgence in the digital age, radio has been a conduit for narrative magic, weaving tales that ignite the imagination and forge emotional connections with listeners across the globe.

A JOURNEY THROUGH TIME: THE EVOLUTION OF RADIO STORYTELLING

Radio storytelling traces its roots back to the early 20th century when pioneers like Orson Welles and the Mercury Theatre brought drama and suspense into living rooms with productions like "The War of the Worlds." These early broadcasts showcased the potential of radio as a medium for immersive storytelling, captivating audiences with vivid soundscapes and compelling narratives.

The Golden Age: Radio Drama Reaches Its Peak

The 1930s and 1940s marked the golden age of radio, with serialized dramas, mystery thrillers, and comedy shows dominating the airwaves. Programs like "The Shadow," "The Lone Ranger," and "The Adventures of Sherlock Holmes" transported listeners to distant worlds and thrilling adventures, fostering a sense of communal engagement and anticipation.

Radio as a Cultural Catalyst

Beyond entertainment, radio served as a cultural catalyst, shaping public discourse and fostering a sense of unity during times of crisis. From Franklin D. Roosevelt's fireside chats to broadcasts documenting pivotal moments like the moon landing, radio became a trusted source of information and inspiration, bridging geographical divides and fostering a sense of collective consciousness.

The Decline and Resurgence: Radio in the Digital Age

As television gained prominence in the mid-20th century, radio dramas waned in popularity, giving way to music-centric formats and talk radio. However, the advent of podcasts and digital streaming platforms sparked a resurgence of interest in audio storytelling, providing a new frontier for creators to explore innovative narratives and reach diverse audiences.

The Power of Imagination: Why Radio Endures

What sets radio storytelling apart is its ability to engage the imagination in ways that visual mediums cannot replicate. By relying on sound alone, radio invites listeners to co-create the narrative, filling in the gaps with their own imagery and emotions. This participatory aspect fosters a deeper sense of connection and investment in the story, making each listening experience uniquely personal and immersive.

The Future of Radio Storytelling

As technology continues to evolve, the future of radio storytelling holds boundless possibilities. From interactive audio experiences to immersive binaural soundscapes, creators are pushing the boundaries of what is possible, blurring the lines between reality and fiction to craft compelling narratives that resonate in an increasingly fragmented media landscape.

In conclusion, radio remains a timeless medium for storytelling, transcending generations and technological advancements to touch hearts and minds around the world. Whether through gripping dramas, thought-provoking documentaries, or whimsical comedies, radio continues to captivate audiences with the power of the human voice and the limitless potential of the imagination.

THE BIRTH OF PODCASTS FROM RADIO

The birth of podcasts can be traced back to the traditional radio broadcasting landscape. While radio has been a staple medium for delivering news, entertainment, and information for over a century, the rise of podcasts represents a natural evolution of audio content consumption in the digital age.

Early Roots in Radio

Before podcasts emerged as a distinct medium, radio shows were already experimenting with on-demand and downloadable content. Many radio stations offered listeners the option to stream or download past episodes of their favorite shows, allowing for greater flexibility in consumption. This laid the groundwork for the on-demand nature of podcasts.

Pioneering the On-Demand Model

The term "podcast" itself is a portmanteau of "iPod" and "broadcast," highlighting its origins in the early 2000s when Apple's iPod revolutionized portable media consumption. As digital audio players became more prevalent, individuals and organizations began experimenting with creating their own audio content, distributing it online for listeners to download and enjoy at their convenience.

Shaping the Podcast Landscape

Radio personalities and broadcasters played a significant role in shaping the early podcast landscape. Many radio hosts and producers saw podcasts as an opportunity to reach new audiences and engage with listeners in a more intimate and personalized way. They leveraged their existing platforms and fan bases to launch podcasts, covering a wide range of topics from news and politics to comedy and storytelling.

Democratizing Audio Content Creation

One of the key differences between radio and podcasts is the accessibility and democratization of content creation. While radio broadcasting typically requires significant infrastructure and resources, podcasts can be created by anyone with a microphone and an internet connection. This has led to a proliferation of diverse voices and perspectives in the podcasting space, catering to niche audiences and underserved communities.

Expanding Reach and Audience Engagement

Podcasts offer creators unparalleled flexibility in content delivery and audience engagement. Unlike traditional radio broadcasting, which is bound by programming schedules and geographic limitations, podcasts can be accessed anytime, anywhere, and by anyone with an internet-enabled device. This has enabled podcasters to reach global audiences and foster deep connections with listeners through personalized content and interactive formats.

Driving Innovation and Experimentation

The transition from radio to podcasts has sparked innovation and experimentation in audio storytelling and production. Podcasters have embraced new formats, storytelling techniques, and distribution channels, pushing the boundaries of what is possible in audio content creation. From narrative-driven series to immersive soundscapes and interactive experiences, podcasts continue to evolve and adapt to changing audience preferences and technological advancements.

In conclusion, while podcasts have roots in traditional radio broadcasting, they represent a distinct and dynamic medium that has democratized audio content creation, expanded audience reach, and fostered innovation in storytelling. As podcasts continue to grow in popularity and influence, they serve as a testament to the enduring power of audio as a medium for communication, education, and entertainment.

USING STORYTELLING TO GROW YOUR BRAND

In today's digital age, radio and podcast storytelling offer powerful avenues for growing your brand and connecting with your audience on a deeper level. Here's how:

Building Authentic Connections

Podcasts and radio shows provide a platform for authentic storytelling, allowing you to share your brand's journey, values, and mission in a compelling and relatable way. By sharing personal anecdotes, behind-the-scenes insights, and interviews with team members, you can humanize your brand and foster genuine connections with your audience.

Demonstrating Expertise

Utilize radio and podcast storytelling to position your brand as an authority in your industry or niche. Create content that educates, entertains, and inspires your audience, showcasing your expertise through thought-provoking discussions, interviews with industry leaders, and in-depth analyses of relevant topics. By providing valuable insights and information, you can establish credibility and trust with your listeners.

Creating Engaging Content

Radio and podcast storytelling offer a versatile platform for creating engaging content that resonates with your target audience. Experiment with different formats, such as narrative storytelling, interviews, panel discussions, and audio documentaries, to keep your content fresh and captivating. By understanding your audience's preferences and interests, you can tailor your content to meet their needs and keep them coming back for more.

Expanding Your Reach

Podcasts and radio shows have the potential to reach a wide and diverse audience, allowing you to expand your brand's reach beyond traditional marketing channels. Leverage social media, email marketing, and guest appearances on other podcasts to promote your episodes and attract new listeners. Additionally, consider collaborating with influencers, industry partners, and guest experts to tap into their existing audiences and broaden your brand's exposure.

Fostering Community Engagement

Radio and podcast storytelling create opportunities for building a community around your brand, where listeners can connect, engage, and interact with each other. Encourage audience participation through listener feedback, Q&A segments, and interactive polls, fostering a sense of belonging and loyalty among your audience. By nurturing this community, you can turn listeners into brand advocates who champion your message and support your growth.

Measuring Impact and ROI

Track key metrics such as listener downloads, engagement rates, and conversion rates to measure the impact of your radio and podcast storytelling efforts. Use analytics tools and listener feedback to gain insights into what resonates with your audience and refine your content strategy accordingly. By continuously evaluating and optimizing your approach, you can maximize the return on investment (ROI) of your brand storytelling efforts.

In conclusion, radio and podcast storytelling offer powerful opportunities for growing your brand, building authentic connections with your audience, and establishing your brand as a trusted authority in your industry. By leveraging the unique strengths of these mediums and creating compelling, engaging content, you can elevate your brand's visibility, reach, and impact in the digital landscape.

THE POWER OF RADIO STORYTELLING IN BUSINESS MARKETING

Radio has been a staple of mass communication for over a century. Despite the rise of television and digital media, radio remains a powerful medium for storytelling and marketing. The auditory nature of radio makes it a unique platform for businesses to create memorable stories that resonate with listeners. This chapter explores how radio storytelling has been successful for marketing a business, highlighting specific examples and strategies that have proven effective.

The Power of Audio Storytelling

Radio storytelling leverages the power of audio to paint vivid pictures in the listener's mind. Unlike visual media, radio requires listeners to use their imaginations, which can create a deeper and more personal connection to the story.

This engagement is particularly valuable for marketing, as it can make a brand more relatable and memorable.

Case Study 1: Coca-Cola's "Happiness Factory" Campaign

One of the most successful examples of radio storytelling in marketing is Coca-Cola's "Happiness Factory" campaign. This campaign created a fictional world inside a Coca-Cola vending machine, where magical creatures worked tirelessly to produce bottles of Coke. The radio ads brought this world to life with detailed soundscapes and engaging narratives.

Strategy and Execution

1. **Character Development:** The campaign introduced a cast of whimsical characters, each with distinct personalities and roles within the vending machine. These characters helped to personify the brand and made the story more engaging.
2. **Sound Design:** The use of sound effects and music was crucial in creating the immersive world of the Happiness Factory. The sounds of machinery, laughter, and the bustling activity inside the vending machine made the story vivid and engaging.
3. **Consistent Narratives:** Over time, the campaign released multiple radio ads that continued the story, creating anticipation and keeping listeners engaged with the evolving narrative.

Impact

The "Happiness Factory" campaign was a huge success, leading to increased brand loyalty and higher sales. Listeners connected with the characters and the magical world, associating those positive feelings with the Coca-Cola brand.

Case Study 2: Warby Parker's "Buy a Pair, Give a Pair" Story

Warby Parker, an eyewear company, used radio storytelling to promote their "Buy a Pair, Give a Pair" program. This initiative promised that for every pair of glasses purchased, the company would donate a pair to someone in need. The radio ads featured real stories of individuals who had benefited from the program.

Strategy and Execution

1. **Real-Life Stories:** The ads featured testimonials from people who received glasses through the program. These personal stories highlighted the impact of Warby Parker's mission and made the campaign more relatable.

2. **Emotional Appeal:** The storytelling focused on the transformative effect of receiving glasses, emphasizing how it improved recipients' lives. This emotional appeal resonated with listeners and motivated them to support the cause.
3. **Call to Action:** Each ad ended with a clear call to action, encouraging listeners to visit Warby Parker's website and make a purchase. The connection between the story and the listener's potential impact was clear and compelling.

Impact

The "Buy a Pair, Give a Pair" campaign not only boosted sales but also enhanced Warby Parker's brand image as a socially responsible company. The stories of real people benefiting from the program created a strong emotional connection with listeners, driving both brand loyalty and sales.

Case Study 3: GE's "The Message" Podcast

General Electric (GE) ventured into long-form audio storytelling with their science fiction podcast, "The Message." This podcast was a serialized story about a group of cryptographers trying to decode an alien message. While not a traditional radio ad, this podcast showcased how businesses can use storytelling to engage audiences.

Strategy and Execution

1. **Engaging Narrative:** "The Message" featured a compelling storyline that kept listeners hooked across multiple episodes. The narrative structure encouraged binge-listening, keeping the audience engaged over time.
2. **Subtle Branding:** While the podcast was primarily entertainment, it subtly incorporated GE's brand by highlighting their technology and innovation. This approach kept the branding from being intrusive while still associating the story with the company.
3. **High Production Quality:** The podcast's professional sound design, voice acting, and scriptwriting set a high standard for audio storytelling. This quality production made the podcast enjoyable and credible.

Impact

"The Message" was a critical and commercial success, reaching millions of listeners and earning positive reviews. It demonstrated that GE was an innovative and forward-thinking company, enhancing their brand image in a unique and memorable way.

Radio storytelling has proven to be a powerful tool for marketing, allowing businesses to create emotional connections with their audience through engaging narratives. The success of campaigns like Coca-Cola's "Happiness Factory," Warby Parker's "Buy a Pair, Give a Pair," and GE's "The Message" podcast illustrates the potential of this medium. By leveraging the unique strengths of radio storytelling, businesses can create memorable experiences that resonate with listeners and drive marketing success.

Chapter 7

How to Use Podcasts to Sell Your Product!

Elizabeth Gearhart and Richard Gearhart

Podcasts continue to gain importance as a marketing tool for businesses. In addition to traditional marketing channels, podcasts add a new means for customers to find a business and/or product. Podcast directories add an additional roster of searchable internet sites to a business's online presence, reaching a different audience than traditional channels. Apple and Spotify are the most listened to podcast platforms, but there are many others as well, and each of them has a business subdirectory in their lists of podcasts.

Recent research shows that 62 percent of Americans have listened to a podcast, and listeners come from most age groups, with 66 percent of the audience in the 12–34 age range. The United States has the most listeners, with 40 percent of Americans tuning in monthly. Statista predicts that listenership will be over 100 million people in the United States in 2024.

According to Wired Clip, over 50 percent of listeners are influenced by podcast ads, and are more likely to buy a product after hearing an ad for it on a podcast. Wired Clip also reports that 45 percent of podcast enthusiasts have household incomes over $250,000.

How are businesses using podcasts to sell their products?

1. Business owners or representatives are promoting their products on podcasts hosted by others that cater to a consumer audience.
2. Business owners are starting their own podcasts where they offer education or other valuable content.
    a. If a business owner doesn't have a YouTube presence, a podcast can be used for YouTube content.
3. Placing ads on podcasts or using in-podcast promotions.
4. Taking advantage of affiliate marketing.
5. Repurposing podcast content for social media.
6. Adding the logo or link to the podcast they appeared on under the 'media' section of their websites to build their presentation portfolios.

How are law firms using a podcast to help their clients sell their products?

1. Hosting a podcast that showcases clients' companies.
2. Hosting an educational podcast and inviting clients to appear as experts.

HOSTING A PODCAST

Business owners are finding podcasts that fit their market by networking, both in person and online, for instance on LinkedIn, and by registering on sites like Podmatch and Guestio. When one registers on matching sites, they'll be asked questions so that they can be matched to appropriate podcasts based on their area of expertise and topics. Once a match is made, a guest will be given detailed instructions on when, where, and how to join the podcast. There may be a pre-call for the host to connect with the guest and clarify details about the show.

Often podcast guests are asked to provide a list of talking points or relevant questions that the host can ask them. The guest can use online tools such as Answer the Public to find questions of interest to the public related their business, then script their talking points to include these questions. We highly recommend that any speaker whose content will be used digitally does this. The reason is for Search Engine Optimization (SEO) purposes so that the internet search engines will find their content.

During the podcast interview, the business owner is usually given enough time to promote their product and explain it in detail, to give their website URL, information on how to find them on social media, and so on, as well as any discount codes for the audience. Although most podcasts are audio, video podcasts are gaining in popularity. These are excellent vehicles to demonstrate how a product is used and to display branding.

Most podcast hosts have a robust promotion campaign for their podcasts that includes a social media component, so the business owner will have visibility on networks that they may not have access to otherwise. The host usually posts show notes as well and will include links to the guests' websites or social media. In addition, some hosts follow their guests on social media and ask the guest to follow them in return; this also expands the guests' social media reach.

Expanding a social media network benefits a small business owner in many ways. Some hosts prefer to offer speaking opportunities to those with larger social networks in the expectation that the guests will promote the podcast to their networks. In addition, the business owner may use Shopify or other tools to sell directly to the public from their social media accounts, so expanding the social media network through podcast networking can be very beneficial.

BENEFIT OF HOSTING A PODCAST

When a business owner hosts their own podcast, it positions them as an authority in their field. It gives them credibility with others and an avenue to use to be invited onto other podcasts. Hosts also develop a media portfolio that can be used to obtain speaking opportunities on other media, such as television. It also generates content that can be uploaded to YouTube, which is very important for online visibility.

Hosts who are selling a product have varying options for their podcasts.

- They can host or co-host a podcast where they discuss topics relevant to their industry. For instance, if one sells lawn sprinkler systems they can host a series of discussions on lawn health, home maintenance, problems to troubleshoot, and so on.
- In an interview type podcast, hosts may interview experts who have knowledge relevant to their broader industry. To use the preceding example, a host who sells sprinkler systems may invite an expert on air conditioner maintenance onto their show, and they may talk about spring startups and winterization for both their products. The interview style podcast leads to networking and sales opportunities, as the host can find experts through Podmatch, Guestio, LinkedIn, or other social media, who can be a source of referrals.

Hosting a podcast is time intensive and many business owners have assistants to help. Important factors for a podcast are content, audio quality, and consistency. Many recording devices deliver adequate quality that can be improved through editing software, but we recommend using a good microphone. We address tips for good content later in this section. Whether a podcast is released weekly, monthly, or on another time frame, it must be consistently released. At Gearhart Law, we host two podcasts. One is released every two weeks, and the other is released monthly, on the same day of the week and at the same time for every episode.

How long should a podcast be? Most podcasts range in length from ten minutes to an hour or more; there are "flash" podcasts, which are very short, but these are typically updates. Although most podcasts are between 20 and 40 minutes, there is no optimum length, although listeners like consistency in the length. The length should be enough to generate the content that is of value to your listener. If a host wants to release their podcast on a frequent basis, they tend to keep the content shorter.

When one hosts a podcast, it's uploaded to a distribution site such as Buzzsprout, Castos, Libsyn, or other, and an RSS feed is generated. There is a monthly fee for each of these platforms. Most sites like Buzzsprout and Castos are for audio podcasts, whereas Libsyn can distribute video podcasts. An RSS feed is basically a link to send a podcast's content to multiple platforms. When a podcast is uploaded to a distribution site, one can choose which platforms to send the RSS feed to.

To illustrate, if a host decides to distribute their podcast using Buzzsprout, during the set-up process a screen appears with a list of platforms asking which ones to transmit the RSS feed to, for instance, Apple Podcasts, Spotify, Amazon

Music, iHeart Radio, Listen Notes, and many others. When the podcast is subsequently uploaded to Buzzsprout, it's automatically distributed to the other chosen sites. Although podcasts are associated mainly with audio, video podcasts are gaining in popularity. Apple and Spotify now have video podcasts, as does YouTube. If using a video distribution platform like Libsyn, the video RSS feed is sent to sites that host video, and the audio RSS feed is sent to audio-only sites.

YouTube is an important platform for anyone who is selling a product or providing a service, as it is the second most searched engine after Google. Google has spent years developing and refining techniques to serve content to a target audience, and it does the same for YouTube. Uploading a podcast to YouTube podcasts has many advantages, such as inclusion in YouTube Music, improved search features, and others.

YouTube added YouTube Podcasts in 2022 and made a change in 2024 to allow podcasters to transmit audio feed to YouTube Podcasts. A static image is generated to go with the audio content. Therefore, even if a podcast is audio only the owner can still take advantage of YouTube's wide reach. If a business owner doesn't have a YouTube presence, a podcast can be used for YouTube content.

It's estimated that YouTube reaches 2.5 billion people. YouTube recently announced that it's testing a powerful new artificial intelligence tool to translate videos into multiple languages, which it plans to roll out soon to all creators.

Podcasts are also valuable for generating social media content. Descript.com is used by many podcasters for editing and pulling out social media clips. Opus.pro pulls out social media clips and gives an SEO, or Search Engine Optimization, score for each clip.

To start a podcast, we recommend incorporating marketing from the beginning. Since the podcast is based on selling a product, the topic has already been chosen. The name of the podcast should include a keyword and the content should be directed to the host's target audience. Whether it's a solo podcast or an interview type of podcast, the host should research questions that people are asking on Google. We use Answer the Public but there are others, or one can type the topic into Google and see the results. Once the host knows what questions to address, they should ask them, even if it's a solo podcast. They can say "customers are asking . . ." and then answer the question. If it's an interview podcast, they can ask the guest. This helps with Search Engine Optimization so the Google algorithms will find and deliver the information.

What kind of content should one use for a podcast? Any content that would answer questions the public is asking related to your industry, or that is of interest in your industry. Many podcast topics are the same as blog topics. If one has a blog already, that content can be turned into a podcast.

In the case study at the end of this chapter we'll review detailed steps of how a person would start a podcast and use it to sell a consumer product.

1. Podcast ads are paid advertising. They usually run 15–30 seconds or 30–60 seconds depending on where in the podcast they're placed, and the costs vary depending on the podcast popularity, length of the ad, placement in show, and so on. You can ask the host to record them, record them yourself, or have a voice-over artist record them. You can even have the host do an on-air endorsement, which is typically more expensive than other ads. Since podcast hosts are typically trusted by their listeners, this can be a powerful tool for selling your product. There are many companies that will help you develop the ad, choose the best podcasts to place it in, and help you measure the effectiveness of your ads, all for a fee, of course.

   A business owner can set up their own ad on many of the podcasting platforms, and it's fairly straightforward. There are YouTube videos on how to generate and post an ad, and with artificial intelligence available now many of the platforms can generate an impressive ad. For instance, to generate an ad on Spotify, a business owner can create an account and follow the steps to place an ad. This follows the steps of many digital advertising tools, where the amount to spend over a given period is decided, and the software helps ad creators with audience targeting, advertising objectives, measurement, and creative tools. The business owner can create the audio script for the ad or ask the platform's artificial intelligence to generate it. When the ad is created and paid for, Spotify will place the ad on podcasts that the software predicts will attract your target customers.

   What makes for a good audio ad? There are many types of ads, some humorous, some serious, and so on. At Gearhart Law we like using testimonials from our clients, and we ask them to say the name of their companies in the ad. That way we both benefit. We feel these types of ads are the most powerful for our business, but other types of ads may work better for other businesses. If you need help, the platforms have professionals you can hire, or you can hire from sites like Fivrr or Upwork.

   How effective are podcast ads? According to the Super Listeners 2021 report, podcast ads are the most recalled type of ad—with 86 percent of respondents saying they remember seeing or hearing an ad. Social media and websites trail podcasts with 80 percent and 79 percent respectively.

   According to the same study, podcast listeners also scored high in terms of engagement with ads, as well as responsiveness, with 76 percent of listeners saying they've taken action after hearing a podcast ad, which could include visiting a site, making a purchase, or taking out a subscription.
2. Affiliate marketing is basically a referral service that uses digital marketing. A buyer visits a website or other media and clicks on a link that takes them to a page where they buy a product. In return, the seller pays the

website owner a fee for the referral. Many podcast hosts will have affiliate links on their websites if they host the type of podcast where people discuss products. Oftentimes the host will promote the affiliates in their podcasts as a way to drive consumers to the website. The affiliates must have an affiliate program to track the purchases and to pay the website owners. Many people join an affiliate network to find affiliate partnerships. It helps to have a large online presence, and using a podcast and social media can expand your reach. There are a number of companies that assist with affiliate marketing.

3. Repurposing podcast content for social media. There are a number of software programs that will extract relevant clips from your podcast for posting on social media. One such program is Opus.pro, which extracts a clip and calculates the SEO (Search Engine Optimization) score. SEO is important for being found in internet searches.

   These clips can be edited to add captions that will direct viewers to your website or product page. The length can be tailored for optimization of the platform of your choice, Instagram, Facebook, LinkedIn, YouTube shorts, and so on, wherever the audience for your product gets their information.

   A podcast can generate 3–5 clips per episode, depending on how long it is. Since the host normally asks a question and the guest answers, the clip may be highly ranked for SEO, particularly if they've selected the questions for SEO value prior to the interview.

   This can be a huge time saver for business owners because they can generate quality content about relevant topics with minimal extra effort. They don't have to search for topics or try to record snippets separately. Oftentimes it's much easier to answer a question on a podcast, even though you know it's being recorded, than to stand in front of a camera or phone and try to recite enough content for a social media clip.

4. When a guest appears on a podcast, many will add the name of the podcast to their list of media appearances on their website. This adds credibility to the guest and their product. Many business owners who appear on media will have the logos of the media on their websites. If the guest wants to appear on other media, such as TV or radio, they can point to their presence on podcasts to showcase their media skills.

HOW CAN LAW FIRMS TAKE ADVANTAGE OF PODCASTS TO HELP THEIR CLIENTS?

As podcasts gain in popularity, more people are not only listening but also have a desire to be on a podcast. Starting and producing a regularly scheduled podcast takes a significant amount of time and effort; the most successful podcasters either make it a full-time job or have a number of assistants working for them. That said, people who want to go on a podcast may not understand how the host/guest matching system works and may need someone to invite them onto an established podcast. That's when an attorney who has an interview style podcast can invite their clients to appear as guests on their podcast. The clients have an opportunity to promote their products, and the firm can promote the podcast using the strategies discussed earlier.

Gearhart Law has a radio show and podcast called Passage to Profit, hosted by Richard and Elizabeth Gearhart, where clients are invited onto the radio show to showcase their businesses and products. The show is repurposed as a podcast the day after it airs on the radio. The clients are then highlighted in the show's social media, and they get a link to their websites from the Passage to Profit website. The podcast is embedded on the website and is distributed to a number of podcast platforms, including Apple, Spotify, iHeart, and others. It's also uploaded to YouTube. Many times clients are invited back to give an update on their projects.

Attorneys or firms may host an educational type of podcast for their audience, where they feature firm clients as experts on the topic. The clients can showcase their expertise. Potential customers can find their companies in the episode promotion materials. This is an indirect way to advertise a product, as the focus is on the expertise and not on the product.

David Postolski, Esq., Gearhart Law partner, hosts a monthly event that is released as a video podcast. The event is called the Entrepreneurial Strategy Series, where clients are invited to speak at events to discuss their entrepreneurial journeys. The event has been held monthly since 2020 and has a number of core participants, as well as new participants, and is attended by over 50 people each month.

In conclusion, there are many ways a business owner can use podcasts to sell their product, and many companies that can help them optimize their opportunities. Now is the time to take advantage of this popular business tool.

CASE STUDY

Amy has a business called Barkin' Bites, where she designs and develops a line of dog toys that she sells online through her website and Amazon. She's trademarked the name and logo. She's active on social media; her largest following is with her Instagram account, but she has LinkedIn, Facebook, X, and TikTok accounts. She's thinking about using YouTube but most of her content is written or in the form of short videos. She's interested in YouTube shorts but hadn't used them yet. She's never been on a podcast.

A friend suggested that Amy go on podcasts to talk about her dog toy company to see if she'd like the experience. She registered on Podmatch and created a guest one-sheet, where she filled out an "about" section, the guest details, added her social media handles, guest tags, ideas for a title for her segment, and questions she could answer. Amy wasn't sure what questions she wanted to be asked, so she turned to AI and used ChatGPT to generate the list for her. She added her biography and a call to action. Since Amy hadn't been on any podcasts yet, she couldn't add that to her profile, but she had to start somewhere! The software matched her to shows that she could be on, and she used the built-in messaging tool to connect with the hosts.

Soon Amy was appearing on podcasts to talk about her dog toys, and she found it quite enjoyable. She was able to identify and compile a list of commonly asked questions based on what the hosts asked her, and she found a number of dog lovers on Podmatch. Amy decided she had enough topics and podcast connections to start her own podcast, so she decided to take the leap. Since her podcast is about dogs and toys, Amy decided to produce a video podcast so she could show dogs playing with the toys. The first thing she did was to watch and listen to podcasts about dogs and dog toys. That gave her a good feel for how she wanted to run her podcast. She decided to use Libsyn to host and distribute her podcast since it seemed to have the best features for video podcasts and it was straightforward to connect the RSS feed to Apple Video Podcasts.

Next she needed to decide: just Amy and her dogs with the toys, or interview style, or a combination? Should she get a co-host? She knew she wanted to show videos of the dogs playing with the toys, but she also wanted good audio. Amy decided to do the podcast by herself, introducing a new toy or toys each time. She found out about Capcut, which allows creators to superimpose photos and video over their content. She knew there were other new editing programs being invented, but she liked this one.

Amy was excited to try making the content before she went further, so she recorded herself playing with the dogs with some of her toys. She bought a good microphone that she could use with her phone, then she headed for the dog park. She met another dog mom in the dog park and asked if she would try the toys. The other mom consented, and she even let Amy record her dogs playing with the toys. Afterward she gave Amy a testimonial that she said could be used in the podcast, but she didn't want the video used, just the audio. She said the dogs' video could be shown though.

Amy used her notes from having gone on other podcasts to help her choose topics. She also used Answer the Public and ChatGPT. She used these tools to script questions for herself to answer during the podcast as well.

Amy set up a recording studio in her spare room. She bought a good microphone, headphones for interviews, some bright standing lights, and added sound proofing tiles to the walls. She put the tiles in front and behind her to capture rogue sounds. She put some on the other walls as well. Then she arranged a well-designed background that included her branding and pictures of her dogs and dog toys.

Amy could have used Zoom, but she chose to use QuickTime player on her MacBook to record herself with her dogs while she talked about and demonstrated the toys. Amy used iMovie to splice the video of the dog mom giving the testimonial into her longer video. Once the entire video was done, she uploaded it to Capcut. She separately loaded the videos of the dogs playing with the toys (without audio), which she superimposed over her video. She was able to superimpose the other dog mom's dog video over the testimonial so the woman's voice could be heard but she couldn't be seen. Amy was very happy with her video, and it was about 20 minutes long. The video showed sections of Amy speaking to the camera, then sections with dogs playing while Amy spoke in the background.

Amy decided to keep going. Next she needed a title. She'd learned from a seminar that the title should contain at least one keyword, so she decided to come up with one that started with the word Dog. After some thought, she called it Dogs Destroying Toys. She researched to make sure the name wasn't taken, and found she was good to go!

One thing Amy had to work on was to describe her toys, and the way the dogs played with them, so that someone listening on an audio podcast could picture them. She knew she could direct people to the video podcasts or her Instagram channel, but she wanted to gain subscribers on the audio podcast sites as well as the video sites.

The next project Amy tackled was to design the artwork for her podcast cover (what the public sees when they search podcasts) and her individual episode covers. She looked at many podcast covers and watched videos on how to design the perfect cover, then she tried it on her own in Canva. She even used Canva's AI image generation app, but she wasn't pleased with her design skills so she worked with a designer whom she hired on Fivrr until the cover met her expectations.

Next Amy started a YouTube channel for the podcast. She'd had to start a Gmail account to get the YouTube channel, and she used her podcast name for the account. She had the designer make a YouTube banner and she made a short intro video to pin to the homepage of her YouTube channel. She added YouTube shorts to her social media posting schedule.

Amy added the cover artwork onto the beginning of her video using iMovie, then worked on her Libsyn page. She decided to voice her own introduction and conclusion and to make them short. She chose to connect her podcast feed to all of the podcast platforms that Libsyn offered, and she uploaded her podcast cover and her podcast episode. She didn't make it live immediately, though, because she had read that she should release three podcasts initially. Amy spent a weekend making videos to turn into podcasts and had two more ready to go by Monday. She decided to post weekly after that, so she generated a new podcast every week.

Amy uploaded the three podcasts to Libsyn and made them all live. She also put them on her YouTube channel in a playlist she titled "podcast" and added the playlist to YouTube podcasts. Amy had discovered that YouTube looks at the podcast title for keywords, but, unlike the other podcasting sites, it also looks at the first few lines of the description for keywords. She made sure to pack the description with key questions from the podcast. She also used the AI tool Castmagic.io to generate titles and show notes that she could add to Libsyn and YouTube.

Now what? Now it was time to focus on marketing! Amy used Opus.pro to extract clips from her podcast for social media and added the podcast content to her social media schedule. She also used the Opus clips for YouTube shorts. She found she could get about three good clips from each podcast.

Amy kept going on other podcasts and meeting more dog moms and dads, and she decided to invite some of them onto her podcast. Although she kept to the initial premise of the podcast by showing at least one new dog toy each time, and answering a question about dogs, she let others talk about dog clothes, food, best doggie hotels, and so on. If she introduced a brand-new line of toys, Amy still did a solo podcast so she could devote enough time to her own business.

Amy decided to set up a separate website for her podcast, so she used Podpage, where she could organize all of her episodes. This gave her yet another place on the internet for Google and other search engines to find her company, as well as other dog lovers. She was also able to use Podpage's affiliate program.

Amy included other affiliate programs on her main website. The other dog parents invited her to sell her products through their websites, and she put their products on her site. Every time someone used her site to find and buy a product from another dog parent, Amy got a commission. She also found affiliates through forums and affiliate channels. And every time Amy got a sale through an affiliate's site, she paid them a small amount.

One more opportunity afforded itself to Amy. She hired a publicist and was able to appear on radio and TV shows with her dog toys. She used her podcast as a steppingstone to other media opportunities.

Soon Amy found she couldn't do it all, so she hired a virtual assistant to help with everything but the content generation and forming relationships with other dog lovers. This gave Amy time to do what she loved best, play with her dogs, meet other dog lovers, create toys and run her company, and tell the world about it all through her podcast and other media.

RESOURCES

ChatGPT – research source
https://chat.openai.com/
Fivrr – general assistance contractors for hire
www.fiverr.com
Upwork – general assistance contractors for hire
www.upwork.com
Canva – DYI design
www.canva.com
Capcut – DYI online editor
www.capcut.com

Descript – DYI online editor
www.descript.com
Answer the Public – SEO terms
https://answerthepublic.com/
CastMagic.io – titles and show notes
www.castmagic.io

REFERENCES

- https://prioridata.com/data/podcast-statistics/
- www.statista.com/topics/3170/podcasting/#topicOverview
- https://wiredclip.com/podcast-statistics/
- www.thepodcasthost.com/listening/podcast-industry-stats/
- www.adresultsmedia.com/news-insights/ultimate-guide-to-podcast-advertising/#Is%20Podcast%20Advertising%20Effective
- www.listennotes.com/search/?q=passage%20to%20profit&scope=podcast
- www.coursera.org/articles/affiliate-marketing
- http://support.podpage.com/en/articles/8597938-all-about-podpage-s-affiliate-program
- https://recurpost.com/blog/youtubestatistics/#:~:text=With%20a%20reach%20of%202.5%20billion%20people%2C%20YouTube,second%20most%20popular%20search%20engine%20after%20Google%20%28obviously%29.
- www.buzzsprout.com/blog/how-long-should-a-podcast-be
- https://support.google.com/youtube/answer/13175969?hl=en#zippy=%2Cwhy-should-i-distribute-my-podcast-to-youtube
- https://ads.spotify.com/en-US/
- www.tomsguide.com/news/youtube-is-getting-a-powerful-ai-dubbing-tool-heres-how-it-works

Chapter 8

Shark Tank Waters

Swimming, Sinking, and Succeeding

Yannis Moati

INTRODUCTION

Have you ever booked a hotel room just for a few hours? Many people haven't, yet by noon, nearly 65 percent of hotel rooms sit empty, representing a multibillion-dollar opportunity wasted every day. That untapped market, full of underutilized real estate assets, was the driving force behind HotelsByDay, a company I built to disrupt conventional hotel bookings and make rooms accessible all day, every day. Do away with the anachronistic and rigid check-ins/outs. But our path to success wasn't a straight line. This is the story of how swimming in the *Shark Tank*, nearly drowning in a sea of rejection, ultimately ignited a series of resourceful decisions that led to our triumph.

PART I: THE BRINK OF FAILURE

1: The Tumultuous Beginning

February 2016: a month synonymous with disaster for HotelsByDay. One year after launch, the situation was dire, far worse than we initially thought. The bank account was barren, strategies were flopping, and the stack of unpaid bills on my desk threatened to block out the skyline. Cofounders weren't showing up at the office anymore. Early investors either gave up on their investment or kept pushing for a miraculous pivot. We were facing significant challenges that went beyond the surface-level issues. On the verge of bankruptcy, the unthinkable seemed worth considering.

2: From Travel Expert to Tech Novice

I'm Yannis Moati, HotelsByDay's fearless (and very much foolhardy) captain, founder, and CEO. Travel was my lifeblood for 20 years. Tours, agencies, I'd cut my teeth in the industry. But tech? Tech was a completely different domain, with its own unique challenges. That first year was a brutal initiation.

Projections soured, hotels balked. Board meetings morphed into battlegrounds. My founding team—the people I'd put my faith in—abandoned ship. Doubts persistently troubled me. Then the lifeline I never expected. Not an investor, not a lifeline deal . . . customer calls. Guests raved—the service, the freedom. They craved more HotelsByDay. Their enthusiasm pierced the despair. I couldn't let them down. That simple shift—that's when I resolved to fight back.

PART II: TURNING TIDES

3: A Ray of Hope in Dark Times

This isn't just about a failing startup. Entrepreneurs often face desperation and resort to unconventional strategies to turn things around. Those customer calls were a beacon in the storm. Grasping at any hope, I dove headfirst into superstition. Chinese New Year, a giant dragon . . . . Look, I'm not one for lucky charms, but when you're in a desperate situation, you'll take any opportunity that comes your way, even if it's risky. So when an entrepreneur friend suggested we try that tradition—stuffing a red envelope with money into the mouth of a giant dragon for a little luck—I figured, why not? I did something I never did before: leave the office midday and have a sense of resignation to let the chips drop where they may.

4: The Dragon's Luck

Believe it or not, as I walked away from that dragon, with my red envelope full of hopes and dreams in its jaws, the next thing you know, an email was on top of my inbox: *Shark Tank*. We'd said no to those guys before. The show seemed too flashy, misaligned with what we sought to be—a "serious business" image. However, desperation breeds flexibility. The *Shark Tank* invitation presented itself as an opportunity, albeit a daunting one.

PART III: THE SHARK TANK GAMBLE

5: Desperate Decisions

The entire team's mindset changed completely. Survival wasn't enough anymore. And that taught me a valuable lesson: money isn't a problem anymore when you have a strong goal that the team can rally around. This was a slingshot toward national exposure, a chance to put HotelsByDay on the map. The clock was ticking, four months "till pitching to the Sharks" (showtime was much later and definitely not guaranteed). My team? They rallied, focused on that singular goal. Frantic energy replaced despair.

We aimed for a flashy pitch, something memorable with music and a bit of flair. . . . Looking back? We were rushing, convinced our idea alone would carry us through. A rookie mistake, fueled by misplaced confidence.

Expectations were building up rapidly, creating a sense of anticipation and pressure. Part of me believed we'd conquer those Sharks. Our platform was ready to explode, a revolution waiting to happen. But investors hammered home a brutal truth: control. Don't become shark food. Day by day we slowly shifted our minds toward which Shark we wanted in and which we should refuse their offers. Sip by sip, we were drinking the Kool-Aid.

So, we went in high—a crazy valuation. Was it self-defense, or a way to guarantee failure and keep our freedom? A gamble, either way. It wasn't just exposure on the line; it was the fate of HotelsByDay.

Even with everything hanging in the balance, the *Shark Tank* invitation ignited a flicker of hope. We wondered if this could be our chance to turn things around.

6: The Fallout of Exposure

The *Shark Tank* stage is an intimidating environment that can highlight weaknesses and challenge even experienced professionals. Walking that dreaded hallway towards the stage, adrenaline surges, panic lurks just beneath the surface. I usually bluff the "confident extrovert" routine, but not there. The bright lights, cameras, and scrutinizing gazes of the Sharks created an intense atmosphere.

My colleague Brian, the smooth talker. He froze. Cue the awkward silence. Not exactly how we'd practiced it. Our little song-and-dance routine—meant to break the ice—unfortunately backfired, leaving the Sharks more puzzled than amused. Then came the attack.

Those Sharks don't mess around. Questions like machine-gun fire, barely a breath between them. I had to forcefully shout: Stop, stop!. . . which they did and the room silenced for a few seconds, enough to catch my breath and mentally, imaginatively, raise a sword to slay a few of these beasts. Kevin O'Leary, the one I feared most, surprised me. He was brutal, but it was a conversation, not a bloodbath. He actually listened and asked questions that followed a certain logic. Turns out, he wasn't just calling us idiots (though maybe he thought it). He pinpointed the HotelsByDay weakness—once the big guys saw our success, they'd copy us, crush us.

Now, Chris Sacca? The stuff VC nightmares are made of. This guy backed innovation, so we had hope. Instead, he was dismissive, condescending. All those horror stories about egotistical investors? Yeah. When he jumped ship first, that was the death knell. Like a domino effect, the rest followed, and just like that, it was over.

PART IV: AFTERMATH AND LESSONS LEARNED

7: Public Failure, Private Lessons

Walking off that stage . . . the feeling was undeniably difficult to process. Defeated, humiliated, the knowledge of our failure echoing on national TV. We felt overwhelmed by the realization that our failure was broadcast on national television. Brian and I had to pull ourselves together for the exit interview. I was shaking, fighting back tears. Not ashamed to admit it. This wasn't a business deal gone wrong; it was our dream publicly shattered and potentially aired to millions of viewers.

8: The Unexpected Upside

But the nightmare wasn't over. Despite our disastrous pitch, the *Shark Tank* spotlight had twisted consequences. People flocked to HotelsByDay out of morbid curiosity, I guess. A double-edged sword for sure. Succeed, and they likely air your segment once.

But stumble spectacularly like we did? You find yourself becoming a recurring punchline. "Maybe if we had a good show, it would have only been featured once instead of, you know, 20 times in the last six years. . . . Ego trip and ego-wise, terrible, but business-wise possibly the best outcome: no shark investment and 10X the potential visibility."

The humiliation of our *Shark Tank* failure was a gut punch. But in that wreckage, I found the most valuable lessons—ones that would shape everything that followed.

PART V: REBUILDING AND RESILIENCE

9: Rising from the Ashes

The Shark Tank rejection felt like more than just missed funding. It was like our idea itself had been publicly flogged. I'd warned investors about bad deals, so money wasn't the core issue. The glimmer of optimism we held was extinguished . . . the belief that HotelsByDay could ignite Shark-worthy excitement. The public humiliation compounded our financial woes, feeding a wildfire of self-doubt.

The aftermath? Like waking from a nightmare into a worse one. For 24 hours, Brian and I were shellshocked. The thought of returning to New York, facing my wife, my friends, our investors, and everyone who supported us in this process with the truth of our failure . . . almost too much to bear.

You have to understand: We pitched that *Shark Tank* guaranteed success so hard and so convincingly that the Kool-Aid spread and we quickly moved into the hallucination world, where we already were talking about the future partition of the spoils of the upcoming treasure: which provider with back-payments will be paid first, which new provider we'll sign up with, who we'll hire for tech, marketing, who will get extra shares for their past support for no financial contribution. I was even looking for new office space. That's how far the collective hallucination went.

Managing the business with severe limitations became the standard operating procedure. Pushing financial obligations to their limits and depending on unpaid interns who ultimately drained more resources than they saved—it was a frantic effort driven by pure determination.

Ironically, that modest stipend was the first money I'd seen in a year. Tiny silver lining, but a reminder: even in total disaster, there are always those tiny glimmers. But even amidst the wreckage, a spark remained. It would take time to reignite, but the lessons learned in that *Shark Tank* disaster would pave our path forward.

10: New Strategies and Newfound Strength

Initially, the *Shark Tank* spotlight had a sickening uncertainty to it. "We weren't sure if we were going to be aired or not. So there's very little I could do. And again, with little money. It's your limit anyway, even if you had big plans." The lack of immediate return was brutal, the inability to act agonizing.

But with time, as we pivoted with ideas like FlexBook, the much-sought pivot that investors were asking for: merging our day stays inventory with night stay inventory, to provide the guest the possibility of guaranteed early check-in and/or late check-out to their multiple night stays.

The lessons learned on that stage started to click. Not the Sharks' business advice, but the sheer grit it took to walk away and keep fighting. Interestingly, the public embarrassment served as a strong catalyst for innovative thinking.

The aftermath of *Shark Tank* was a baptism by fire in resilience. Confronting that public setback and then returning to the demanding realities of running a business—it challenged everything I thought I knew. It also taught me to never, ever quit, to find ways to innovate even in the bleakest moments.

We kept building the business, making lemonade out of lemons; we pitched our partner hoteliers that we'll be airing on *SharkTank* and to sign up to our collection and possibly advertise as well prior to the airing, for maximum visibility. Turns out quite a few did, and we slowly replenished our coffers. Mixed in with that was the fact that we shared all the structural fat from being in the financial furnace for over a year, then we quickly and unexpectedly turned profitable.

Shark Tank may not have ignited the growth I envisioned, but it forced a mindset shift that was crucial to HotelsByDay's survival. Feeling stunned by the experience, the process of reconstructing our marketing strategy seemed like a daunting undertaking.

But with newfound resilience, we got to work, even within the television show's contract constraints that held us back.

PART VI: MARKETING AND MOVING FORWARD

11: Creative Constraints

After our episode finally aired (the suspense was its own form of torture!), we slammed into the reality of that *Shark Tank* contract. Turns out, you can't plaster their logo everywhere and scream, "The Sharks loved us!" So, we tiptoed the line: a tiny picture of us pitching, an "As Seen on *Shark Tank*" next to it. Maybe we were too timid. Turns out, others got away with flashier stuff. . . .

Did *Shark Tank* change our marketing strategy? At first, no. Demoralized and broke isn't the recipe for creativity. But that looming airdate was a kick in the pants. Suddenly, we were scrambling to make sure our website wouldn't crash from the traffic surge we desperately hoped for. Pro bono SEO help, upgraded servers—we did what we could to look ready for our fleeting moment in the spotlight.

And then we pulled a rookie move. The actual *day* our episode aired—our website registration expired. Site down, not from a crush of customers, but because we forgot to renew our URL registration. It wasn't set on automatic renewal. After all, why should it be, as we were penniless and one New York minute away from bankruptcy? Talk about embarrassing. Yet, there was a bizarre twist . . . we saw a bookings spike. People assumed our site was down due to massive demand. FOMO played to our favor.

12: Turning Chaos into Opportunity

Shark Tank taught us some hard lessons about strategizing (not so much about marketing). Mostly about being operationally ready for anything. We could have found ways to use that exposure, even with the contract restrictions.

But it did push us to think about how powerful TV can be, even when the appearance itself is a disaster. The *Shark Tank* spotlight brought visibility, but it was up to us to turn that attention into something lasting. Our goal? Craft a new brand narrative built on that chaotic, unforgettable TV moment.

13: The Moment of Truth

That February week in 2017, when our *Shark Tank* episode aired . . . It was madness. Neighbors waving and shouting, "Hey, I just saw you on TV!" The excitement in their voices was a jolt, and honestly, a bit overwhelming.

I had people stopping me on the street saying that they saw me . . . it was really weird. Being in New York, a city full of entrepreneurs, I guess it shouldn't have been a surprise that I was getting recognized. But it wasn't just the ego boost (though hey, there was a bit of that). Suddenly, the show's massive reach hit me, and how it catapulted HotelsByDay into the spotlight.

We hustled to capitalize on the *Shark Tank* exposure, even within those tight contract limits. "As Seen on . . ." splashed across the homepage. A press release hinted at skyrocketing demand. It was about survival, about crafting the perfect narrative.

14: The Rollercoaster of Reactions

The hotel industry wasn't shy about their opinions. One memorable email from a Boston property suggested that HotelsByDay had no value, echoing the Sharks' opinions. That stung.

Ouch. But I'm nothing if not stubborn. I fired back an email, sparking a dialogue. They softened slightly, but no deal. Yet on the flip side, a chain reached out because of the show, eager to partner and capitalize on the visibility. Shark Tank swung open those doors, for better or worse.

The show was a blessing and a curse for our brand. Sure, some reactions stung, and deeper pockets would've meant bolder marketing. But the exposure sparked conversations we desperately needed, lending credibility even amidst the snark. Suddenly, HotelsByDay wasn't just a concept; we had a story. That story turned heads and got people talking.

Looking back, our *Shark Tank* ride was a crash course in entrepreneurship—the glorious highs, the brutal lows, and the moments so absurd they were hilarious. I walked away with battle scars and invaluable lessons any potential contestant needs tattooed on their brain before stepping foot in that arena. But through it all, I learned hard lessons that the opportunity isn't so much about pitching to investors, but rather being TV material for the public's need of bread and circus.

PART VII: REFLECTIONS AND ADVICE

15: Lessons for the Future

If I could go back and tell myself one thing before walking into that TV studio, it would be know who you're pitching to: Shark investors, or public audience? Who do you want to convince? Those Sharks, just like any investors, have seen way too many bad pitches and have a knee jerk reaction to say no.

So maybe the next time, the idea isn't about convincing anybody, but rather taking the opportunity to talk about the business you created, the vision you can lie down and rally your team around. Here's the thing most people don't get: if you're not going in there with the main goal of getting funded, then you need a different strategy. *Shark Tank* is entertainment. Thrives on drama. Memorable moments mean your segment gets replayed over and over. That's visibility right there.

So, you have two options: Nail your pitch, be so sharp they have nothing to criticize . . . *or* go down in flames (metaphorically). Neither guarantees you a deal, but both make you unforgettable. And that means eyeballs on your website. Because people can't resist a good trainwreck, or a stunning victory.

Too many people think getting on *Shark Tank* is about the money. Sure, investment is nice, but the true goldmine is the eyeballs it puts on your business. And the way to maximize that exposure isn't by playing it safe. Ignite controversy—be the genius who wows them, or the one who gets utterly shredded. Make them remember you.

"Do not misconceive this *Shark Tank* experience as a funding opportunity. This is a TV audience public viewership opportunity. So create as much of a clown car as you can, as much drama as you can."

Underestimate the power of *Shark Tank*, and you do so at your peril. Play your cards right, even without securing a deal, and it's a publicity explosion capable of transforming your business.

Shark Tank lit a fire within me that still burns brightly. But understanding the true meaning of "success" after such a whirlwind experience required deeper reflection. . . .

16: Redefining Success

This was a wild ride, a defining moment in my business journey. It hammered home a hard truth: no matter how good your idea is, how prepared you think you are, something will always throw you off. I didn't get coaching before going on, a smugness in me thinking we were smarter than the average *Shark Tank* pitch. What a colossal mistake. If I could do it over, I would rehearse relentlessly and maybe even hire a coach to drill me for that level of scrutiny.

Did *Shark Tank* make us successful? The honest answer: it's hard to say. Our business wasn't the kind where someone watches TV and immediately books a room—it required research, planning. Plus, TV fame fades fast, and our competitors may have benefited more long-term due to having better rankings on Google than we did back then.

The truth is, there wasn't a magic bullet from *Shark Tank*. Startups are a marathon, not a sprint. Our *Shark Tank* appearance helped, but the real lesson was this: be ready for anything, capitalize on exposure, but know it's not a magic fix.

Shark Tank is a masterclass in resilience, a brutal reminder to always be learning. We didn't score the fairytale ending, and that's okay. Launching a company and running a startup will make you face some unknown experiences and challenges. . . . *Shark Tank* is definitely right there on the top of experiences and environments that you're not trained for. The key takeaway isn't the money, it's how you grow from the gut-wrenching pressure.

Our TV appearance may have been a disaster, but the fallout taught us invaluable lessons. Looking ahead, we're determined to translate those lessons into a future where HotelsByDay dominates the daytime booking space: resilience, no matter the odds. If you like what you do, then money is an afterthought.

PART VIII: LOOKING AHEAD

17: Goals and Gratitude

Our goal remains the same: to become the uncontested leader in the daytime booking space despite facing stiff competition. This business has been a roller-coaster, but it's only made us more determined to innovate and succeed.

18: A Changed Perspective

Shark Tank changed me. I learned that setbacks aren't just obstacles, they're fuel—but only if you choose to harness them. Our *Shark Tank* experience was an immersive education in entrepreneurship—marked by incredible successes, painful challenges, and moments that were so unexpected they bordered on comical.

If I could rewind the clock, I'd obsess over preparation. Coaches, rehearsals, worst-case scenarios—"I'd prepare for the worse, instead of confidently thinking of the best outcome."

The irony isn't lost on me. Back then, I thought "bombing" on *Shark Tank* was my downfall. Turns out, those reruns did more for HotelsByDay than any flawless pitch ever could. Ego took a hit, but business boomed.

My journey, and the *Shark Tank* part of it, are proof that sometimes the best opportunities come when the plan fails spectacularly. That keeps getting hammered home as we keep growing this business. And yeah, the fact that our *Shark Tank* episode is still famous, all these years later? That fuels a whole other kind of motivation.

PART IX: CONCLUSION

19: From Disaster to Growth

Empty hotel rooms during the day, real estate assets not optimized—a problem I was determined to solve with HotelsByDay. The road to *Shark Tank* was brutal, fueled by desperation and sleepless nights. But facing those Sharks, that's the gamble every entrepreneur must consider to reach new heights.

Here are some key takeaways for entrepreneurs considering braving the Tank, or just navigating the tumultuous waters of a startup:

- **Don't Sweat the Numbers:** Give a broadline and keep it to a few single KPIs. Maybe my lesson was that I spent too much time thinking of every possible number thrown my way and none of them came up. It was all about the concept and the vision.
- **Embrace the Chaos, Exploit the Exposure:** *Shark Tank* is a spectacle, not just a pitch. Whether you succeed or spectacularly fail, it thrusts you

into the spotlight. Have a plan to capitalize on that visibility, even if it means pivoting your marketing strategy.

- **Surviving the Spotlight:** Whether you score a deal or not, be ready. The episode airs, and chaos descends. Have a plan to handle the crush of traffic, inquiries, and the spotlight's heat.
- **The Cycle of the Startup:** *Shark Tank* is a sprint; entrepreneurship is a marathon. Each stumble, each triumph—learn from them. Because the greatest comebacks are built on the scars of past defeats.
- **Navigating Success and Setbacks:** There's no linear path; it's full of switchbacks and wrong turns. The show taught me the grit a startup needs, and how to dance with the unpredictable beast that is business.
- **The *Shark Tank* Effect:** A double-edged sword: it's a spotlight, but it fades fast. The true power lies in using those fleeting minutes to fuel long-term growth through brilliant marketing and relentless focus on your customers.
- **Remember Why You Started:** When the pressure mounts and the doubts creep in, remember the passion that sparked your business. Setbacks are inevitable in a startup. What sets you apart is the ability to bounce back, learn from failure, and forge ahead even stronger.

Shark Tank wasn't the fairy tale I'd envisioned, but it was a school of hard knocks. It taught me the value of resilience, the value of failure as well: as you can easily spot who is important, who is loyal, and what is important to keep in the midst of a financial drought.

Shark Tank was a single chapter in a far bigger story. Those lessons, the publicity—it all fuels our journey now. We're out to redefine daytime bookings, and the *Shark Tank* experience is an extra feather in our cap, an eternal icebreaker; it's now part of our culture of grit, part of the reason we won't fail.

And looking back to it, it was a blessing in disguise: getting funding from the Sharks at such a young age of our business, with no North Star, no trained team, no financial stability, would have been a costly victory and there would have been no HotelsByDay to talk about today.

About the ABA Section of Intellectual Property Law

From its strength within the American Bar Association, the ABA Section of Intellectual Property Law (ABA-IPL) advances the development and improvement of intellectual property laws and their fair and just administration. The Section furthers the goals of its members by sharing knowledge and balanced insight on the full spectrum of intellectual property law and practice, including patents, trademarks, copyright, design, and trade secrets. Providing a forum for rich perspectives and reasoned commentary, ABA-IPL serves as the ABA voice of intellectual property law within the profession, before policy makers, and with the public.

Books from the ABA Section of Intellectual Property Law (ABA-IPL)

AMERICAN BAR ASSOCIATION
Intellectual Property Law Section

Title	Regular Price	ABA-IPL Member Price
ADR Advocacy, Strategies, and Practices for Intellectual Property and Technology Cases, 2nd Ed. (5370231)	$149.95	**$119.95**
ANDA Litigation, 3rd Ed. (5370243)	$379.00	**$295.95**
Antitrust Issues in Intellectual Property Law, 2nd Ed. (5370263)	$149.95	**$119.95**
Arbitrating Patent Disputes (5370229)	$89.95	**$74.95**
Biosimilars Litigation and Client Counseling (5370267)	$169.95	**$139.95**
Careers in IP Law (5370204) (The ebook is complimentary with ABA-IPL Section membership)	$24.95	**$16.95**
Commercialization of IP Rights in China (5370241)	$119.95	**$95.95**
A Comprehensive Patent Practice Form Book (5370260)	$139.95	**$109.95**
Computer Games and Immersive Entertainment, 2nd Ed. (5370239)	$89.95	**$69.95**
Copyright Litigation Strategies (5370228)	$369.00	**$285.00**
Copyright Remedies (5370208)	$89.95	**$74.95**
Crash Course on U.S. Patent Law (5370221)	$39.95	**$34.95**
The DMCA Handbook, 2nd Ed. (5370234)	$79.95	**$64.95**
The Essential Case Law Guide to PTAB Trials (5370233)	$249.95	**$199.95**
The Essentials of Japanese Patent Prosecution (5370245)	$149.95	**$119.95**
Intellectual Property and Technology Due Diligence (5370236)	$219.95	**$179.95**
The Intellectual Property Law Handbook, 2nd Ed. (5620154)	$139.95	**$109.95**
IP Protection in China, 2nd Ed. (5370270)	$149.95	**$119.95**
IP Strategies for Medical Device Technologies (5370238)	$149.95	**$119.95**
IP Valuation for the Future (5370237)	$89.95	**$59.95**
The Law of Trade Secret Litigation Under the Uniform Trade Secrets Act, 2nd Ed. (5370242)	$369.95	**$295.95**
A Lawyer's Guide to Section 337 Investigations before the U.S. International Trade Commission, 5th Ed. (5370266)	$139.95	**$109.95**
Legal Guide to Video Game Development, 2nd Ed. (5370227)	$74.95	**$59.95**
A Legal Strategist's Guide to Trademark Trial and Appeal Board Practice, 4th Ed. (5370247)	$179.95	**$144.95**
Marketing Your Invention, Product, or Journey, 4th Ed. (5370271)	$59.95	**$47.95**
New Practitioner's Guide to Intellectual Property (5370198)	$89.95	**$69.95**
Patent Claim Drafting Practice (5370259)	$179.95	**$144.95**
Patent Freedom to Operate Searches, Opinions, Techniques, and Studies (5370230)	$139.95	**$109.95**

Title	Regular Price	ABA-IPL Member Price
Patent Litigation Strategies Handbook, 5th Ed. (5370269)	$425.00	**$340.00**
Patent Trial Advocacy Casebook, 3rd Ed. (5370124)	$149.95	**$119.95**
Patently Persuasive (5370206)	$129.95	**$99.95**
The Practitioner's Guide to the PCT, 2nd Ed. (5370261)	$139.95	**$109.95**
The Practitioner's Guide to Trials Before the Patent Trial and Appeal Board, 3rd Ed. (5370258)	$169.95	**$139.95**
Pre-ANDA Litigation, 3rd Ed. (5370256)	$349.00	**$259.00**
Preliminary Relief in Patent Infringement Disputes (5370194)	$119.95	**$94.95**
Principles of Patent Claim Drafting and Patent Claim Analysis (5370268)	$159.95	**$127.95**
Right of Publicity (5370215)	$89.95	**$74.95**
Settlement of Patent Litigation and Disputes (5370192)	$179.95	**$144.95**
Starting an IP Law Practice (5370202)	$54.95	**$34.95**
Summary of Covenants Not to Compete (5370244)	$179.95	**$144.95**
The Tech Contracts Handbook, 3rd Ed. (5370248)	$42.95	**$33.95**
Trademark and Deceptive Advertising Surveys, 2nd Ed. (5370255)	$189.95	**$151.95**
What Is a Copyright, 4th Ed. (5370257)	$19.95	**$16.95**
What Is a Patent, 4th Ed. (5370262)	$19.95	**$16.95**
What Is a Trademark, 5th Ed. (5370254)	$19.95	**$16.95**
What Is a Trade Secret (5370265)	$19.95	**$16.95**

Find these and other ABA-IPL books at ShopABA.com

Thank you for your order!

Jeff Salyards
Executive Editor, ABA Publishing
jeff.salyards@americanbar.org

Tax, shipping and handling charges may apply.
See web store for complete details and current shipping and handling rates and information.

2 EASY WAYS TO ORDER **ShopABA.org** OR **(800) 285-2221**